Recipe For a Dream

Orangebooks Publication

1st Floor, Rajhans Arcade, Mall Road, Kohka, Bhilai, Chhattisgarh 490020

Website: **www.orangebooks.in**

© Copyright, 2024, Author

All rights reserved. No part of this book may be reproduced, stored in a retrieval system, or transmitted, in any form by any means, electronic, mechanical, magnetic, optical, chemical, manual, photocopying, recording or otherwise, without the prior written consent of its writer.

First Edition, 2024
ISBN: 978-93-6554-673-6

RECIPE FOR A DREAM

By Arjun Freeman

OrangeBooks Publication
www.orangebooks.in

I Dedicate This Book to My Precious, Whose Love and Support Made This Book Possible, And to My Family. I Also Dedicate It to My Favourite Teacher, Who Inspired Me to Persevere Through Difficult Times.

Introduction

―――◆―――

Dreams, dear dreams
Angelic princesses
Without your presence on earth
The world would be still and empty.

You are the butterflies raised by angels of heaven.
You guests from the heavens,
Without my consent,
You unlock the doors of my mind
And paint with seven hundred colours
Without a canvas - like rainbows.

~ Vayalar Ramavarma ~

Dreams are a kaleidoscope of visuals, emotions and ideas brought into existence by the coming together of random neural connectivity and subconscious thoughts. It is an ethereal, fluid state of mind where the impossible becomes possible, the boundaries of reality are blurred, and the mind is free to explore the depths of its own desires, fears and hopes.

In this work, I share how certain dreams have changed my perception of life, leading me to become less self-centred, more mindful, and more aware of the complexity and beauty of existence. Through these dream-induced revelations, I found the motivation and strength to navigate the challenges of life and find my way to greater understanding and fulfilment.

Dreams are a universal phenomenon that have captivated the human imagination for centuries. They occur in a certain state of consciousness during the sleep cycle, and are characterised by vivid sensory, cognitive, and emotional experiences. The exact function and purpose of dreams are still not fully understood by scientists, but some theories such as the psychoanalytic theory by Sigmund Freud, have tried to define dreams as a manifestation of unconscious desires and conflicts, providing a window to our conscious mind.

The cognitive theory of dreaming developed by J. Allan Hobson and Robert McCarley suggests that the brain's random neural activity during sleep is transformed into the vivid visions that make up our dreams. It states that random neural activity is the primary source of dream content. It is widely accepted as an explanation for the purpose and function of dreaming.

Another interesting theory by Calvin Hall suggests that dreams can help us find solutions to problems by allowing us to think creatively and outside the box.

By analysing these theories together, we can say that dreams are a unique blend of memories, subconscious thoughts, and the brain's ability to process information and create visions. It is a complex interplay between the different aspects of our being, reflecting our deepest desires, fears, and hopes, as well as our capacity to create, reason and solve problems.

Dreams can be seen as a form of mental escape, providing a sense of freedom from the constraints of daily life. They can offer a space where we can explore our thoughts, emotions, and experiences in a more imaginative and creative way, free from the limitations of reality. Some people believe that dreams can reveal unconscious desires and repressed emotions, providing insight into one's inner self and helping to promote personal growth and self-awareness. Everyone can have their own views on the meaning of dreams.

From a scientific perspective, dreams are a neural phenomenon. They are a natural part of the sleep cycle and are thought to be the result of activity in the brain.

Dreams are therefore a real and complex phenomenon that involve the activation of multiple brain regions and can have a significant impact on our emotional experiences and well-being.

While some dreams may be fleeting and forgettable, others can have a lasting impact on our thoughts, emotions, and behaviours. It is this potential for personal growth and self-discovery that makes dreams such a valuable and endlessly fascinating aspect of human experience.

Some people find meaning in their dreams and use them for self-reflection and growth, while others may not find them significant. But I compiled some of the dreams I had and wrote this book because they gave me the inspiration to persevere in my pursuits in life and I wish to share those.

It is up to you to follow or forget a dream which you had, but it is important to remember that they can be a source of inspiration and creativity.

Content

1. Introduction v
2. The Beginning 1
3. The Pen 2
4. The Word 7
5. The Normal 25
6. The Food 48
7. The Dance 62
8. Free Will 74
9. Fire And Flame 86
10. The Tree 91
11. The Surrender 98
12. The Lover 102
13. The Puzzle 110
14. The Dream 122

The Beginning

There was a long-tailed star that lived in the vastness of the sky.

He wished to fulfil someone's wish before he burned into dust.

She was looking at the sky through her window

And saw the long-tailed star, and she made her wish with joy:

She wanted the falling star for herself.

To make your wish come true was I born, but where are you?

The Pen

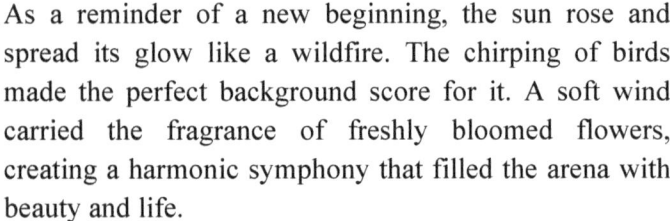

As a reminder of a new beginning, the sun rose and spread its glow like a wildfire. The chirping of birds made the perfect background score for it. A soft wind carried the fragrance of freshly bloomed flowers, creating a harmonic symphony that filled the arena with beauty and life.

Meanwhile, I was snoring on the bed and enjoying a beautiful dream. As the warm rays of the morning sun peeked through the windows, my mother's voice suddenly echoed in the room, "Wake up, it's time for school."

I awoke from the beautiful dream but, not yet ready to face the day, I rolled over and muttered, "Amma, just five more minutes, I'm lost in a dream too lovely to let go of."

But my mother wasn't ready to take any of it. She pulled my blanket down, shook my legs and said, "No way! It's already late. Get up!"

I kicked myself free of my blanket and groaned, "Okay, Okay. I'm up."

With a warm glow in her eyes and a gentle smile on her lips, Mom said, "Get up and chase your dreams."

She reminded me of the adventures that lay ahead of me and how I could conquer the world.

I was so excited to get to school that day because my father had given me a special pen and I wanted to show it off to my peers. I arrived at school a bit later than usual due to the unexpected rain. When I entered the classroom, the teacher asked me, "Why are you late?"

"Sorry, Ma'am. I missed the bus due to the rain."

"Okay. Take your seat. No more disruptions." Although the teacher scolded me for being late, I couldn't help but feel a sense of excitement as I pulled out my new pen and began taking notes. The pen emitted a low electronic sound as it powered up, catching the attention of my classmates.

They started whispering to me, "What's that? Can we see it?"

They were curious about the strange pen.

I explained, "It's my new pen, gifted by my father. It absorbs carbon from the atmosphere and converts it into ink. The ink used in this pen has been made from pollutants in the atmosphere. The pen is able to absorb and convert it into ink." I couldn't help talking in class but felt a sense of pride as I explained to them about it. I continued, "Not only does this mean that the pen can write for longer, but it also helps to reduce the carbon footprint in the atmosphere."

The teacher saw us whispering in the middle of her lecture and headed straight for my seat. She yelled, "What's going on here?", causing me to feel frightened.

Suddenly, I felt someone tugging at and pulling my blanket off. There stood my mom, shouting at me to wake me up. I awoke from my dream.

Mom hollered, "Wake up! It's time for school."

I complained drowsily, "Amma, you ruined a beautiful dream where I was gifted a special pen that saves the environment." I was still in slumber. I rolled over and said, "Five more minutes, Amma."

With a warm glow in her eyes and a gentle smile on her lips, Mom said, "Get up and chase your dreams."

That day, I headed off to school inspired with a new sense of purpose. The whole day in school, I couldn't shake off the image of the pen from my mind. I spent the day thinking about my dream and how I could make it come true. The dream felt so real and the pen seemed so unique and innovative. I couldn't help but feel a sense of longing to hold such a pen in the real world. I found myself constantly wondering what the dream could have meant. As the day went by, I couldn't ascribe any clear meaning or significance to the dream, but it filled me with a feeling of inspiration and a desire to find ways to make a positive impact on the environment.

The idea of using technology to reduce carbon emissions by inventing a pen that converts atmospheric carbon into ink is certainly mind blowing. But it would require enormous research and technological advancements to make this concept a reality. Right now, such a technology does not exist and designing such a complex machine that would fit inside a pen is nearly impossible.

Even if we succeed in developing such a pen, what would be the cost of the pen!

Although inventing a pen that can directly convert carbon into ink may be an impossible task, a feasible alternative is to cultivate algae and extract ink from them. Algae produces more than half of the earth's atmospheric oxygen. They also have several desirable characteristics sustainable for ink production, including fast growth, diverse colours, and the ability to grow without the use of fertilisers, herbicides, or genetically modified seeds. There are a few companies working on extracting ink from algae that are cultivated in a controlled environment. This ink can be used for printing on paper, cardboard, and textiles. It is 100% biodegradable and can be disposed of in a compost pile, where it will degrade in just a few days. Algae-based ink is a promising eco-friendly alternative to traditional ink.

Dreams are personal and can have multiple interpretations. Some may interpret the dream of being gifted a technologically advanced pen as an impetus to follow the dream and make it a reality, and thereby solve the problem of global warming through technological innovation. But there could be other interpretations too.

After learning and understanding more about dreams, I interpreted the dream about the pen from a philosophical perspective. A pen could be used as a weapon to bring about positive changes in society. Just as, with every word I wrote, the pen in the dream cleansed the atmosphere of carbon, the words we pen down can also cleanse the society of its pollutants. The pen, as a tool that recorded and shared knowledge throughout history, has the power to shape societies and cultures. Even today, it is still worth using the same tool.

The pen is a tool that can be used to explore and express our thoughts, opinions and emotions. These expressions can inspire and bring change in readers. This book is an experimental attempt at using one of the most powerful tools ever known to humankind. I'm dedicating myself as a pen in the hands of consciousness to use me for writing a new version of its story.

And while a pen does not judge what the author writes, but simply feels the ups and downs when we use it to write, in the end, the work of a pen could be a masterpiece. So just forget about judgements and just flow!

Thanking all my gurus for teaching me how to use the most powerful weapon.

~Sarvam Samarpayami.

The Word

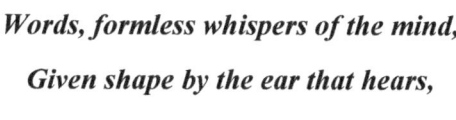

Words, formless whispers of the mind,
Given shape by the ear that hears,
Breathing life, they grow and thrive.

Words can heal or harm,
A miracle, constantly shifting form,
With each ear that they reach.

Insight is the key for perceiving,
The word within the word,
So, look within and you'll find,
Words that can set you free.

~Inspired from poem "Vakku" By Joji Kuriakose~

The word is the creator and the word is the creation.
A word is not just a simple unit of language, but a complex and multifaceted phenomenon that encompasses various dimensions and layers of meaning. Its study requires an interdisciplinary approach that takes

into account linguistic, semiotic, cognitive, cultural, historical, pragmatic, social, psychological, philosophical, ethical, and metaphysical dimensions.

Words can strike like lightning and protect from thunder. Words are shaped by the mind that receives them.

The mind uses words to organise its thoughts, feelings and each word we utter has specific connotations in our mind. For the same word can have dual meanings, with positive and negative implications. The same word can evoke different feelings and emotions depending on the context in which it is used and the listener's personal experiences and cultural background.

Over time, words can gain new meanings and connotations. The evolution of words is a complex and ongoing process that can be influenced by a range of factors, including scientific and technological advancements, socio-political changes, and the infusion of new ideas and concepts.

For example, the word "vulgar" originates from the Latin term "vulgus," meaning "the common people." The term shifted in meaning during the Renaissance when the idea of "high culture" emerged, coming to refer to something that is considered crude, unrefined, or lacking in good taste. Today, the word "vulgar" is often used to describe behaviour or language that is considered offensive, inappropriate, or lacking in refinement.

The evolution of words and their connotations highlights the dynamic and changing nature of language, and this evolution of words is often referred to as the 'semantic shift'. This means that the definitions of words are not set in stone, and can change and evolve over time, leading to new or altered meanings.

Words do not define anything, but are merely symbols or labels that we assign to things, and they do not have any inherent meaning. The Swiss linguist Ferdinand de Saussure proposed that the meaning of words is arbitrary and based on conventional or agreed upon usage, rather than any inherent qualities of the things they represent. In other words, the meaning of a word is determined by the way it is used in a particular language community, and not by any objective, universal properties of the thing it refers to.

"Water" is a noun that refers to a clear, colourless, odourless, and tasteless liquid that is essential for most forms of life. "H_2O" is a chemical formula that represents the molecular composition of water, with the letters H and O representing hydrogen and oxygen respectively.

Linguistic conventionalism refers to the practice of using words and symbols in a specific and agreed-upon manner to represent concepts, objects, or ideas. In this case, "water" is the conventional term in everyday language used by English speakers to refer to the substance, while "H_2O" is the conventional scientific notation used by chemists and other scientists to represent water at the molecular level.

So, the colour of the sky can be changed if we change the name of the colour. This means if we start addressing the "blue" colour as "green", the name of the colour changes and that can change the name of the colour of the sky. The word is simply an elusive entity accepted and agreed upon by the majority for interacting within the same community.

Now think about this. If you had a truly one-of-a-kind experience, how would you convey its essence to someone else in a way that allows them to understand and appreciate its significance?

We may be able to explain what happened but the listener may not understand it till they get a taste of the same experience. Words can be a powerful tool for communication, but such communication is invariably hindered by the limitations in the ability of the listener to understand the experience and ability of language to convey the uniqueness of the experience. Communication can be a powerful tool, but it is often limited because listeners may struggle to fully understand and words may not capture the full uniqueness of an experience.

Similarly, when it comes to communicating emotions, words are often not enough to fully convey the emotions being felt. The true essence of an emotion is often difficult to capture and, as a result, people may resort to nonverbal cues such as facial expressions, body language, or tone of voice to convey the emotions they are feeling. These nonverbal cues can provide important context and help to convey the emotions more effectively than words alone.

For example, When I was a child, I had a painful wound on my knee and I assumed that others would feel the pain if they touched it. I asked my mother to touch my knee, hoping that she would feel the pain I was experiencing. After she touched the wound, she claimed to feel the pain. I believed at that time by having others touch the wound, they could truly comprehend the pain. However, I came to realise my belief was wrong as I grew older.

I learned that the only effective way to communicate our feelings to others is through words. Successful communication relies upon expressing ourselves verbally and the empathy of those we communicate with. This realisation highlights the crucial importance of understanding the limitations of language when it comes to conveying unique personal experiences, pain, and emotions.

Human communication evolved from gestures to spoken language due to the development of the brain and vocal apparatus. Language also developed with culture, society, and technology. The modes of human communication will continue to evolve in the future to enable a better understanding of the people around us.

Words Nurtures Generations

Words are nutrition to the mind, like food to the body. We are very susceptible to the power of words in the early stage of our lives. When we were children, our parents and other adults in our lives used language to define and shape our identities, including our names, character traits, and beliefs, all of which played a role in constructing our image about ourselves. These foundations built on words last as long as we live and reflect in our personality.

If a child is consistently told that they are "stupid" or "lazy", they may internalise those beliefs and develop a negative self-image. This can lead to a lack of motivation and self-esteem and can negatively impact their academic and social development.

On the other hand, if a child is praised for their efforts and told that they are capable and intelligent they are more likely to develop a positive self-image. Which can lead to increased motivation and self-esteem. A study conducted by Mueller and Dweck found out that the children who were praised for their efforts had a higher self-esteem and were more likely to attribute their success to their own abilities rather than external factors.

The words used by parents during early childhood can also shape a child's understanding of their identity and place in the world. For example, if a child is consistently told that they are "different" or "not like other kids," they may internalise those beliefs and develop a sense of estrangement. This can lead to feelings of isolation and low self-worth.

Making fun of children with words can also be hurtful and can lead to feelings of shame and embarrassment. This can negatively impact their self-esteem and confidence, and can make them hesitant to express themselves or share their thoughts and ideas with others. Also, avoid making unrealistic or fake promises to children such as "I'll buy you anything you want, if you do this." This can create unrealistic expectations and disappointment for the kid when the promises are not fulfilled.

When children are compared to their peers or siblings, they may feel pressured to meet unrealistic expectations and may begin to believe that they are not good enough. As a result, they may be less likely to try new things in life or take risks for fear of failure.

From our childhood itself, people belonging to the older generations teach us to fear failures and try to set limits in our minds with words.

For example, people used to say that the sky is the limit, but now the younger generation is proving that the sky is just the beginning. There is a lot more to explore beyond the sky.

In our society, we can see malnourished minds due to the lack of encouraging words. Some people may never have heard an encouraging word in their entire life. This can be due to various reasons such as growing up in a negative or abusive environment, experiencing trauma or neglect, or lacking supportive people in their lives. These individuals may struggle with low self-esteem, self-doubt, and feelings of worthlessness. They may also have a hard time accepting praise or positive feedback from others.

We need to remember that we have the potential to cause change, growth and our kind, encouraging words can have a powerful impact on the self-worth and motivation of people who need it. Encouraging words can help them to feel valued, seen, heard and it can give them the motivation to make positive changes in their lives. It is important for everyone to be mindful of the words they use and to be intentional about speaking words of encouragement and support to those around us.

It is better to be silent when you feel like cursing someone than to make them miserable with your words.

I personally find myself a victim of the words with which my elders, parents and peer group labelled me, making me feel very unlucky and causing me to lack confidence in front of people.

It took me around twenty-five years to understand that I am not defined by external labels. It is important to remember that words don't define you. If someone tries to judge you, it is only an expression of their perception of you. Their judgement is not a definition of you. Only you can define yourself.

No one can fully understand another person completely, but still, they look into other people's lives and judge them. How can people understand others without self-realisation?

Individuals who possess self-awareness and understand themselves tend to be less judgmental of others and more focused on their own goals and responsibilities. They also understand that while it is important to be aware of others' perspectives, we do not need to completely understand someone in order to interact with them effectively.

When someone attempts to judge us, it is important to remember that their opinion is a reflection of their own perspectives and observations about us, not necessarily a definition of who we truly are. It is important to remember that no one truly knows us as much as we know ourselves. The self-awareness can lead to being more thoughtful about our judgments. Everyone is capable of making judgments, but understanding oneself can lead to being more thoughtful about those judgments and the reasons behind them.

But understanding others is an important part of effective communication, building relationships and resolving conflicts. It is not about understanding them to define them, but to understand their perspectives and emotions for better decision making.

Life is to be lived and not to impress others. Everyone can define their own way of success and how to live their own life. No one needs to agree on your own way of defining success, but you should be blissful of being yourself at the moment.

We are already in the prison of the social constructs and conformity imposed on us by the previous generation, but at least let the next generation live a much freer life, a life with confidence in themselves and improvement every day.

Why do we set limits and boundaries for the next generation? Let them explore the world and define their boundaries by themselves.

Encouraging the next generation to be confident in themselves is the best thing we could do for them. When we provide children with quality words that inspire and motivate them, we give them the emotional foundation they need to thrive. We teach them to believe in themselves, to trust their instincts, and to pursue their dreams with passion and determination.

It is important for parents, educators, and society as a whole to use positive and encouraging words to foster curiosity, creativity, and critical thinking in young people. We need to feed them with quality words and behaviour to develop their minds. It is crucial for ensuring that they have the knowledge and skills necessary to make a positive impact on the world and solve the major problems faced by humanity and for the survival of our species.

Word as a Tool for Deception

Words facilitate more privacy in our lives. We can use certain words to convey specific emotions and make the listener believe that it is real even though we might be feeling the opposite in reality. People may use words strategically to create a certain impression or to hide their true feelings.

Jordan Peterson, a Canadian clinical psychologist and professor, has spoken extensively about the concept of truth and lying. He has argued that lying is a fundamental problem in human society and that it is one of the most destructive forces that can undermine trust and relationships. He argues that lying is a sign of weakness and cowardice, and that people who are honest and truthful are more likely to be respected and trusted. Even small white lies, can have far-reaching consequences and can lead to a lack of trust, and that it is important for people to be honest, even when it is difficult. He suggests being truthful, even if it is uncomfortable, instead of telling a lie.

He also emphasised that lying is not only a moral problem but also a psychological one, as it can lead to feelings of guilt and shame, and can cause people to lose touch with their sense of identity and integrity. He encourages people to strive for authenticity, and to be honest and truthful in their words and actions, so as to live a meaningful and fulfilling life.

"Do you remember who lied to you the first time in life?" I asked this question within my friend's circle. They all conveyed that it was their parents who first lied to them, and some of the lies were quite interesting. One friend shared a particular memory where he recalled his mother using a fake blood - coloured substance to stop breastfeeding, which he believed was the first lie he experienced from her. Even at that young age, the child was able to understand that his mother had faked something, left him confused with his first encounter with a lie. It is important to understand that children often learn to lie from their parents. Children may not always be solely responsible for their early experiences with lying.

One notable study in this area was conducted by psychologist Michael Lewis and colleagues in the 1980s. And this research suggests that children may begin to tell lies as early as age 2 or 3, and that lying can be a natural part of development as they learn about social norms and expectations.

Children become increasingly aware of their own thoughts, feelings, and intentions, by the age of 2. This increased awareness can lead to the realisation that they can manipulate the truth to get what they want or to avoid punishment.

We were exposed to the concept of lying or deception in early childhood and this led to the feeling that lying is natural.

If we could visualise all the communication that has occurred throughout human history as a 3D image that anyone could see, it would likely appear highly polluted with deception. It is possible that lying has been present in human communication since the very beginning of time.

We are the victims of words used by the previous generations. Parochial words and beliefs can be limiting and can hold us back from reaching our full potential. Previous generations may have had different cultural or societal norms and values that may not align with our own beliefs and values. This can create conflicts and confusion, and make it difficult for us to understand and express ourselves authentically.

Words can create more walls in our society, so it is important to explore more within ourselves in order to create a more reliable method of communication.

We often believe the words of others to satisfy their emotions rather than probing the truth. That is why many people who believe in words can be easily manipulated. We are living in a society where if we can make others believe a lie, we are perceived as smart, and if we can make a large population believe a lie, we are perceived as powerful. We feel good when people believe in our lies, as we feel smarter than others.

The Future of Words

If we could communicate with different modes, such as through silence and by feeling the emotions of another person, it would be a more effective way of understanding each other's feelings.

In order for society to progress, we need more transparent and trustworthy channels of communication. Lacking transparency and trust in communication can result in negative consequences such as lying and backstabbing.

If telepathy were to become possible, it could revolutionise the way we interact with each other and the world.

I came across the concept of telepathic communication initially from the ancient scripture of Bhagavad Gita.

In the Bhagavad Gita, it is believed that Lord Krishna communicated sacred knowledge to his disciple Arjuna, on the battlefield of Kurukshetra, and provided him with spiritual guidance. Bhagavad Gita has 700 verses in 18 chapters, and it is comprised of the conversation between Krishna and Arjuna. The entire conversation in Bhagavad Gita may take a day to complete. But this conversation is believed to have happened just before starting the war. We cannot think there was enough time to have the entire conversation immediately before the war. Instead, if it was a mind-to-mind communication, it would have taken only a couple of minutes to finish the entire conversation.

During this time Sanjaya, the charioteer of King Dhritarashtra, was blessed with divine vision, which enabled him to witness the events of the battle from afar. Sanjaya had access to this conversation between Krishna and Arjuna. Sanjaya served as the narrator of the Bhagavad Gita, describing the conversation between Krishna and Arjuna to Dhritarashtra.

Here Krishna communicated with Arjuna through their minds, and Sanjaya observed the conversation and communicated it telepathically to Dritharashtra.

When we communicate through the mind, we communicate the feeling rather than the words.

There are different layers of processing involved between our feelings and the words we use to express them. When we communicate with each other, first we have a thought or feeling that we want to convey. This may be an emotion, an idea, or an experience that we want to share with someone else.

Next, we have to translate that thought or feeling into words. This involves a series of cognitive processes, including selecting the right words to use, arranging them in a coherent sentence, and adjusting our tone and body language to convey the intended meaning.

This process of articulating our thoughts and feelings into words is something that we learn throughout our lives. As we grow and develop, we learn new words and phrases, become better at expressing ourselves, and refine our communication skills.

However, if we were to communicate telepathically, we would bypass this process of rendering our thoughts into words. Instead, we would communicate directly using our thoughts and feelings, without the need for language or verbal communication. This would allow us to share our experiences and emotions in a much more direct and intuitive way, without the limitations of language.

Of course, telepathy is currently a theoretical concept and there is no scientific evidence to support its existence. However, the idea of direct mind-to-mind communication has captured the imagination of people throughout history, and remains an intriguing possibility for the future of human communication.

I have had several experiences of telepathic communication within friend circles and family.

The intensity of the experiences was different but the feeling was the same.

One of my experiences was when I was scrolling through my contacts on my phone one day just to give a random call to anyone on my contact list. And I selected a person to call, with whom my previous conversation was a year ago.

I dialled the number and my friend attended and said, "Hi I was just talking about you to my friend and suddenly you called." My friend was from another side of the globe. That was really surprising for me and even to my friend too.

I have had similar experiences with very close teachers, friends and family members too.

When I would be thinking about them, they may give a call or I give a call when they are thinking of me.

I also had similar experiences where, when I was with my friends and wanted to change the music, someone would immediately change the music, with no communication having transpired between us. I shared similar experiences within my friend circle and they said they also had sometimes felt the same way.

These experiences occur randomly, and may not happen when we hope for it or attempt to communicate telepathically.

These experiences are spontaneous and unpredictable, occurring randomly without any conscious effort to communicate telepathically. This is a common characteristic of telepathy, that it cannot necessarily be controlled or summoned at will. I felt that, in these situations, the other person and I got entangled in a single line of thought, and yet it was a random occurrence.

Brain-to-brain communication, also known as direct neural interface or brain-machine interface, is a field of research that aims to develop a system for transmitting information directly between two or more brains. This is done by recording brain activity from one individual and transmitting it to another individual in real-time, bypassing the traditional pathways of speech or written language.

The idea of brain-to-brain communication has been popularised in science fiction, but recent advances in neuroscience and technology have made this a more realistic possibility. It is still in its early stages and more research is needed to fully understand its capabilities and limitations.

A technology-integrated telepathy may result in much transparency and trust.

It could greatly improve communication and understanding between individuals, as people would be able to directly sense each other's emotions and intentions. This could lead to a deeper sense of empathy and understanding between people. It could make it easier to share information and ideas, as people would be able to "telepathically" transmit thoughts and ideas to one another.

Innovations in transparent communication will revolutionise how we understand ourselves and people. Also, we will have more empathy and honesty in our communication.

Conclusion

"Words" and "sword" have the same letters, and both are too dangerous to handle. We need to be more careful about words because it is easy to say something and cause the same impact as a sword. Also, we do not know how the other person conceives the words which we use. They can have a significant impact on the people around us, especially children. It is important to be aware of the power of words and to choose them carefully. Words can be used to build up or tear down, to inspire or discourage, to heal or hurt. They can also be used to shape someone's perception of themselves and the world around them. It is important to be mindful of the words we use and to choose them wisely, with the goal of building up and inspiring others, rather than tearing them down or causing harm.

Saying encouraging words to others is one of the best things we can do for both the individual and the society as a whole. Encouraging words can have a positive impact on a person's self-esteem, self-worth, and motivation. They can also inspire people to reach their full potential and to make a positive impact in the world. It is important to remember that we all have a role to play in creating a more supportive and inclusive society, and that our words can play a significant role in shaping the lives and destinies of those around us.

The Normal

Your words become my cage,

My thoughts, the little bird,

In the inner senses, seeking music of freedom,

I couldn't hear it even during the thunder of monsoon.

Seeming to wake up,

Songs within my soul,

Fluttering like breath in the corridors of memories

Evoke by the hands of muses.

When thousands of people share the same belief, it achieves the status of "normal". But is this so-called normal truly normal or just a fragment of our imagination, perpetuated by those who seek comfort in conformity? People believe in the same notion, but is it because they truly believe in it or out of fear of being different? The search for normalcy is a search for security and belonging.

We must break free from the conventional boundaries of normalcy and embrace our unique essence for true fulfilment and joy. Just because someone does not fit into the societal norm, it does not make them any less valid or valuable. But if someone really rebels against the norms, the society hits back with its toxic words which pierce their minds deeply and then destroy them.

The older generation often tells the younger generation "This is how society works," causing us to forget our dreams and accept it as natural, like birds in a cage assuming that flying is strange.

Sometimes, society can be a cage that limits self-expression and critical thinking. Conformity can lead to a lack of diversity and stifle new ideas, affecting mental health and well-being. When individuals feel pressured to conform to societal norms, they may experience anxiety, stress, and self-doubt. Let's not let society trap us in its cage and forget what an individual is truly all about. Don't be afraid to spread your wings and fly, to question norms, and discover your own definition of life.

Rather than becoming complacent about problems and complaining, let's get frustrated by them and find solutions that benefit both ourselves and the people around us. Thus, we can create a new normal that values and embraces individuality, creativity, and progress for the betterment of humanity.

In order to make things better, it is crucial to have an understanding of how society works. There are different types of truths that shape our beliefs and decisions. The first is objective truth, which refers to facts and information that can be verified through scientific methods or research.

Personal truth, on the other hand, is an individual's subjective experience and understanding of the world, which can be influenced by personal experiences, beliefs, and values.

Political truth refers to ideas that are repeated over time by religions, politicians, corporations, or other groups with an agenda executed through propaganda. While these may not always be true, they can become widely accepted as truth by the general population.

We can promote sustainable living and peaceful coexistence by acknowledging these different types of truths and prioritising the objective truth. It is important to understand the objective truth that underlies our present world in order to create a better future for all.

Discovering the objective truth is an exhilarating journey, diving deep into the enigma of reality. Many individuals have devoted their lives to seeking knowledge and comprehending the truth. However, despite our efforts, the full scope and complexity of our reality remain elusive. Our understanding of reality is not only limited by our senses but also by our cognitive and conceptual limitations. Our brain interprets the signals received by our five senses and constructs our perception of reality.

For example, our eyes can only perceive a narrow range of electromagnetic waves that ranges from 400 to 700 nanometers. We are unable to detect ultraviolet, infrared radiation, X-rays, gamma rays, radio waves, and microwaves. Our auditory range is restricted to frequencies between 20 Hz and 20,000 Hz. We are unable to hear sounds beyond this range. For example, take any other sense organs for that matter. All of them function within a limited range to experience reality. As a whole, we humans have a limited capacity to understand the physical world as we experience it through our senses.

These limitations imply that our perception of reality is incomplete and that we must conduct extensive research and expand our minds to gain a more comprehensive understanding of the truth. We must continue to advance science and technology to uncover the mysteries of reality and should awaken the society as a whole.

We should explore all the possibilities of physical reality, even those that fall outside the limits of our own sensory experience. Because, the discovery of infrared and ultraviolet rays played a crucial role in expanding our understanding of the universe.

Infrared radiation has been a powerful tool in studying the universe, as it can penetrate dust and gas clouds unlike the visible light rays. This has enabled astronomers to study stars, galaxies, and even black holes more accurately.

There are many applications which we developed with the discovery of light waves and sound waves in our daily life. Similarly, we need to continue our exploration to understand the complete version of our physical reality.

Such exploration will change our understanding of ourselves and the world around us. This will lead to the change in what is perceived as normal.

Personal Truth

Personal truth depends on an individual's circle of knowledge and their perception of the world. It is often shaped by socialisation, beliefs, emotions, biases, and personal perspectives. This can evolve over time as a person's experiences and deeper understanding of the world broadens. Personal truth is subjective and unique for each person.

As we strive to understand ourselves and the outside world, we may approach objective truth, but there may be situations were personal truth conflicts with objective truth. In such cases, it is important to be open-minded and accept objective truth. There is no need to debate over it because objective truth is always true whether or not you accept it.

The more your circle of knowledge is closer to objective truth, the more efficient your actions will be. The more unnecessary information you store in your memory, the less efficient your actions will be. The efficient ones are those who can acquire a better understanding of reality and make right judgments and predictions about the situation at hand.

For example: In a situation where there is a 50-50 chance of death or survival, your decision may depend on how logically you process the available information. If your knowledge is influenced by irrelevant information such as; religious or ideological beliefs that are not based on logic, it could potentially lead you to make the wrong decision.

The decisions made in such a critical situation could lead to the extinction of our species if, majority of people's knowledge is based on unscientific and illogical information at a crucial time of mass extinction of the species. Relying on baseless information rather than factual and logical data might hinder our ability to effectively address the challenges and to make informed choices which are necessary for survival.

In such dire circumstances, it becomes crucial to prioritise evidence-based knowledge, scientific understanding, and critical thinking to increase the likelihood of making decisions that are in the best interest of our species and the planet. Being aware of cognitive biases and actively seeking rational, well-supported information can significantly improve our chances of navigating through critical situations successfully. So, the open mindedness towards accepting the objective truths will give us more chances to survive in a challenging situation.

Open-mindedness involves critically evaluating our assumptions to identify any biases or misconceptions that may be influencing our understanding of the world. By doing so, we can constantly learn and grow. It is important to explore all available tools to understand the complexities of reality and use these tools to find out more about the truth. And finally, with that understanding we will be aware and awakened.

Political Truth

Political truth refers to information that is used to support a particular agenda. This information is created by individuals with power and influence who seek to manipulate public opinion. They control major media houses and technologies, shaping the minds of the masses by fuelling fear and greed. Their agenda often involves diverting attention from the truth by promoting unnecessary products and exploiting people's fears and insecurities.

Political parties, organisations and religions have their own agendas which can cloud the objective truth. These groups use various tools to control the masses, shaping our understanding of what is normal and acceptable. Even if someone knows the objective truth, their agents may prevent it from reaching the masses. Sadly, many people crave to know the truth but are unable to penetrate these systems that keep them in the dark.

In this world, there are only two kinds of people: those who are blind and those who are awakened to the truth. For a better world we need a massive awakening to break free from the manipulative influence of political truth and to pursue objective truth.

Science is the Way

We know that science is the only hope to know the objective truth about reality. We need to continuously research in different areas of science to explore more. Even though there are flaws in the way we handle science and technology.

The destructive technology of the atom bomb was developed through scientific research and technology by man himself while lacking ethics in handling the science. Thus, science is often considered to be value-free, since it is based on objective facts and evidence. Along with that it does not involve personal biases or subjective opinions.

The scientific method is structured to reduce bias and uphold the foundation of evidence-based results, rather than relying on personal beliefs or opinions. Nonetheless, some contend that science cannot be completely devoid of values, as the values and assumptions of researchers can subtly shape the course of scientific inquiry. If scientists do not adhere to ethical principles in their handling of information, it could lead to disastrous outcomes.

For example, the choice of research topics, the design of experiments, and the interpretation of data can be influenced by the scientists' personal values and beliefs. The funding and support of scientific research may sometimes depend on societal values and priorities.

So, people like Jordan Peterson argue that science requires something outside of it to guide us for making choices. The values that are used to guide scientific research and decision-making are often referred to as "meta-science" and these values could be ethical, societal, economic and many more. These values should be openly and transparently communicated to the public, whose interests and consent should be incorporated into scientific decision-making. The direction of scientific research should thus be determined based on a shared consensus among the public.

We know that diseases like cancer and diabetes are a major threat to humankind and the research in these areas are a good example of how values and societal priorities should influence the direction of scientific research.

The idea that teaching about food and lifestyle is more important than developing new medicines for diabetes or cancer. This is based on the value that prevention is better than cure. But developing new medicines for diabetes and cancer can generate more profit for pharmaceutical companies and hence they pump more funding in favour of developing medicines rather than educating a healthier lifestyle. If we think in terms of values and social welfare, scientific research should focus more on developing and educating a lifestyle which prevents diabetes and cancer.

The course of scientific research should be shaped by a diverse range of values and societal objectives, and it is crucial to take these considerations into account when determining which research areas to emphasise and how to allocate available resources.

When they developed the atom bomb using science, it led to a new era of fear and mistrust in science and technology. It marked the first time a weapon of mass destruction had been used in war. This event has raised many questions about the morality and ethics of science and technology, and the responsibility of scientists and policymakers in considering the potential consequences of their actions.

The creation and usage of the atomic bomb sparked fear and mistrust in science and technology. For the first time in the history of warfare, a weapon of mass destruction was used. That raises serious questions about morality and ethics in science and technology, as well as the responsibilities of scientists and policymakers. This event prompted a reassessment of the impact of science and technology possess over society, and the need for a greater consideration of the potential consequences of scientific advancements.

Today, the development and deployment of artificial intelligence (AI) presents new ethical concerns, including potential job displacement and economic inequality. As science and technology continue to advance at a rapid pace, it becomes increasingly important to establish a constitution or code of conduct that guides corporations and policymakers in their investments and decisions related to scientific research and development. In order to ensure a more responsible and ethical use of science and technology, it is crucial to balance the benefits of these advancements with the potential risks and consequences to society.

An ethical layer is needed to provide proper directions and focus to science, and it is necessary to have advanced watchdogs to ensure that ethical and moral values are upheld.

We need human and artificial intelligence-integrated hybrid systems for building ethical watchdog organisations. In such systems, the AI component can provide a level of objectivity and consistency in decision-making, while the human component can ensure that ethical considerations are taken into account.

Although AI can be programmed to make decisions based on specific rules and criteria, it lacks the ability for moral reasoning and ethical judgement that is inherent in human decision-making. Therefore, it is important for humans to actively oversee the development and deployment of AI systems and to establish ethical guidelines and standards for their behaviour.

Science and its tools are still young to unveil the true nature of reality. But with this limited understanding we need to define our personal perspective of reality.

We have all asked questions like "Why are we here? What is the meaning of life? What is the purpose of life?" And so on. That is where we can make a difference in our lives.

From my perspective, we are here to eat, love, innovate and show gratitude towards nature and earth systems. These are the four things that keep us alive and moving forward. There is no specific meaning or purpose of life; nothing to do in particular, nowhere to go. It's up to you to choose how you live your life.

We are here to eat: Eating is a fundamental aspect of our existence as living beings. It is essential for the survival and nourishment of our bodies. Therefore, we should educate ourselves about the food we consume and the processes involved in bringing it from the farm to our plates.

It is important for us to aim for well-informed decisions when it comes to our food selection and to actively pursue sustainable and responsible methods in the cultivation, production, and distribution of food. Keep in mind that we are what we eat and our dietary choices have a significant impact on our well-being. So, dedicate ourselves to making wholesome choices for both ourselves and our loved ones and we will never regret it.

If we are not aware of the food we eat, we may fall into a dilemma of misinformation. Corporations involved in the process of food making would profit out of our ignorance and our bodies would suffer as a result. We would be denied the pleasures and nourishment that come from understanding the complexities of our sustenance. By ignoring the importance of learning about food, our plates would be filled with deception and our bodies would become nothing more than a commodity. This could lead to increased rates of malnutrition and diet-related health issues such as obesity, diabetes. Education about food includes awareness about the food that we consume; along with foods that are suitable for our bodies, information about food safety, food storage, and food security. This can also play a critical role in maintaining public health and ensuring the quality of the food served on our plates. Real improvements in the standard of living are achieved through the quality of food we consume. So, educating about food, and getting involved in the process is an essential purpose of life.

We are here to love: Love is a fundamental human experience and emotion that connects us to others, fosters empathy, and brings a sense of purpose and fulfilment to our lives. Love is like a drop of water connecting two sand grains and enriching for sprouting the seeds and growing. The two grains of sand remain deserted and do not support life without the wetness of love.

It gives meaning and purpose to life, to live and let live, this emotion is essential for the continuation of the species and sustaining of humanity. It is the foundation of the family and supports the upbringing of children.

So, we should learn and practice to love unconditionally. Unconditional love can serve as a grounding force. It motivates people to prioritise compassion and understanding in their interactions. Love can give meaning and purpose to life.

We are here to innovate: It is a great purpose as it shows a commitment to continuously improving and finding new ways to do things. It will make us live better than yesterday; our perceptions and thoughts should be better every day by innovating. It also promotes a culture of creativity and experimentation, which can lead to breakthroughs and advancements.

We innovate because it allows us to find new and better ways to solve problems, improve efficiency, and create new opportunities. This helps us to define ourselves. Everyone should be part of it because innovation is not just the responsibility of a selected few. Rather it should be a collective effort. It can involve people from all levels of society; as well as from different backgrounds and perspectives. This diversity of thought leads to more creative and effective solutions.

Continuous innovation is important because it allows us to stay competitive and adapt to changing circumstances. The world is constantly evolving and new technologies, markets, and challenges arise. By continuously innovating, we can stay ahead of the curve and continue to make meaningful contributions to society.

Innovation is not only limited to products or services. We could be innovative in the way we think, communicate or the way we implement our ideas. It is a way to move forward as a person and to improve the lives of the people around us.

Showing gratitude towards nature and earth systems: Showing gratitude towards nature and earth systems is a fundamental purpose of human life because it is essential for our survival and well-being. The earth provides us with the resources and systems necessary for our existence, such as air, water, food, and shelter. Showing gratitude towards these systems means acknowledging their importance and taking steps to protect and preserve them for future generations. It also means recognizing our interdependence with the natural world and understanding that our actions have an impact on the earth's systems. By cultivating a sense of gratitude and respect for nature, we can work towards living in harmony with the earth and ensuring its continued vitality.

During my search for meaning and purpose in life, I found solace and inspiration in science. Particularly, in the realms of quantum mechanics and astrophysics. The theoretical and philosophical implications of these fields have a way of reshaping our self-awareness, the nature and the fabric of our reality. They offer a comforting and profound narrative akin to soothing lullabies.

They simplify the meaning of the world around us and make it easier for us to navigate our lives with clarity of purpose. And these theories helped me find and rebuild myself.

Science is the best way to begin the journey to know about life and reality. This will give you confidence and more freedom to think.

I began with the YouTube videos of Brian Greene, Carl Sagan, Neil DeGrasse Tyson, Greg Braden, Simon Sinek, Osho Rajaneesh, and many other thinkers. Their vision helped me to gain a wider perspective of reality.

When you follow science as an inspiration, you are on the right path.

If you are feeling lost or in need of motivation, I highly recommend turning to science as a starting point. It is an excellent way to explore the world and discover the purpose of life. Science is not only about studying the external world, but also about understanding the internal workings of mind and consciousness.

Science, particularly the study of quantum mechanics has been a profound source of inspiration and motivation for me. The theories and concepts of quantum mechanics are complex and often difficult to understand. But the feeling of having finally grasped them is truly satisfying.

Our brain can be compared to a receptor that engages with the field of consciousness within existence, receiving information that already exists. When we actively seek something, our brainwaves connect with this consciousness field, leading to the generation of new insights. These fresh insights, in turn, are meant for us to analyse and explore further. As long as our quest for knowledge continues, the expansive realm of consciousness offers our brain new stimuli to investigate, creating an endless cycle of exploration.

The so-called 'New Normal'

I started writing this book during lockdown following the COVID-19 outbreak. According to me, pouring my accumulated thoughts into a book may help to engage in something creative.

In India, the lockdown due to the COVID-19 pandemic began in March 2020. This has unleashed widespread panic among the population which led many to self-isolation inside their residence to protect themselves.

For us, this was a 'new normal'. We had never experienced a lockdown in our lifetime before. We had to wear masks in public, practise social distancing and work remotely instead of going to the office and living in constant fear about the situation. We were listening to the news about the amount of people who were getting tested positive for COVID-19.

It triggered panic buying and widespread unemployment and a new strand of chaos emerged from nowhere. No one had any idea about what was really happening.

The media conveyed many things and we blindly believed it. They were informed about a fatal virus out there, which spreads rapidly through the air.

Various perspectives emerged. Some attributing it to human actions while others viewed it as a natural occurrence. A few even cast doubt on the pandemic's existence.

But the majority of people suffered due to the lockdown, not from the COVID virus.

Some business corporations and the governments were testing how to impose a new normal in society by inducing fear in people and controlling the media. Anyhow, the new normal became the reality; the entire population paused their life and sat inside their homes and many people experienced a new way of life. Almost all the people became dependent on the internet for news, remote work, and purchasing things at home.

But why this 'new normal'?

The Story of a Revenge

The deep ocean was filled with despair and hopelessness. Hence, the animals gathered to discuss the destructive impact of humans on the earth's systems. The discussion was led by a wise and ancient whale who had seen the world change over the course of centuries.

The whale began, "My fellow creatures, we have seen the harm humans have brought upon our planet. Their actions have led to the extinction of so many species, the destruction of ecosystems, and the pollution of our waters. We must find a way to stop them before it is too late."

A school of fish joined in, "Yes, we have seen the plastic waste that they throw into the ocean. It is killing us and our young ones. We cannot allow them to continue with this reckless behaviour."

A group of sea turtles added, "We have suffered from their careless fishing practices. They have been taking so much more than they needed and leave nothing for the rest of us. It is not just us, but other creatures on the land also suffer the consequences of their greed."

A seagull, who had flown down from the surface; chimed in, "Their impact is not limited to the ocean. They are cutting down forests, polluting the air, and causing adverse climate changes. We need to do something before it is too late."

The silent dolphin started speaking, "I understand your frustration, but violence is not the answer. We need to find a way to teach them a lesson. What if we work together to give them a warning?"

A sea horse spoke up, "There are only a few of us left in our species. They killed our entire family by their waste dumping and illegal fishing. But how can we make them understand? They seem so indifferent towards our suffering." The sea horse started crying and slowly became angry and screamed, "We should kill them all." All animals joined him and screamed with the seahorse, "Kill them all! Kill them all!"

The ancient whale suddenly interrupted the conversation and said, "Life on Earth started in the sea. Mother Earth supports any life that is fit for survival. That is how all animals have lived till now. We can use our survival instincts not to destroy any species, but to protect ourselves from extinction."

"My forefathers have kept some deadly viruses and bacteria in a vault near the North Pole under the ice. No one has access to them, and they have been kept secret for generations. We can use them in need to protect ourselves and nature from attacks by some species inside or outside the Earth. We can use one of these viruses for our survival.

We could introduce a moderately lethal virus into the human population, causing illness and occasionally resulting in fatalities. The virus will vanish after a certain time and conditions would return to normal. This will be just a warning, but if humans continue to pose a threat to Earth's systems, we can consider mass destruction of the entire human species."

"But one of us will have to carry out this mission."

The animals looked at each other, unsure of who would be willing to sacrifice themselves. Then, a crab spoke up, "I will do it. I have seen enough suffering, and I am ready to give my life to protect our planet."

The animals were touched by the crab's bravery and readied themselves to take the virus. The crab got infected with the virus and swam towards the ocean surface, intentionally getting caught in a fishing net. As he spread the virus among the humans, he whispered to himself, "This is for the greater good."

The crab got caught by the humans and they brought all the harvest to the shore. The infection of the crab spread to the other fishes caught inside the net. After a week the harvest reached the market and from there the virus spread.

This dream, seen during the lockdown period, was an eye opener about the irresponsible behaviour towards nature by humans. The consequences of human actions in the name of progress and development are still being faced not only by our generation, but also pose a threat to those who are yet to come.

I personally believe that the spread of the COVID pandemic was a message from nature that a virus can disrupt all major human activities. It is crucial that we learn from this experience and strive for a better world that benefits us and future generations. We must remain vigilant about the possibilities of more pandemic outbreaks and take proactive measures to prepare for them. During the lockdown, humans stopped all production process and almost all kinds of industrial activities, transportation and construction. This had a good impact on nature. The amount of pollution during the lockdown was very less and this could be observed very clearly.

Since the 1940s, there has been an acceleration of technological growth, leading to widespread exploitation of natural habitats. As a result of global economic growth, the Earth's natural systems have been impacted by the accumulation of carbon dioxide in the atmosphere, acidification of oceans, plastic pollution, and more.

The discovery of fossil fuels was a major factor in the acceleration of globalisation and technological innovation. The generation that lived during the 1940s was primarily driven by the pursuit of profit and growth, resulting in a lack of concern for the long-term consequences of their actions. This greed and ego were deeply ingrained in their behaviour, ultimately leading to the current environmental crisis.

This has unfortunately been accompanied by a significant increase in the deposit of waste and toxins in oceans. This resulted in the destruction of ocean habitats within a century of human intervention. The impact of this activity has been so significant that it led some scientists such as Eugene Stormer and a chemist named Paul Crutzen in 2000, to coin the term "Anthropocene" for this era.

The term "Anthropocene" refers to the significant impact that humans have had on the Earth and its inhabitants. It acknowledges the long lasting and irreversible influence that our species has had on the planet's systems, environment, processes, and biodiversity. This recognition of the magnitude of human impact highlights the need for immediate action to address the environmental crisis.

The Anthropocene marks a period when humans have become the dominant force that shapes the Earth's natural systems including the atmosphere, oceans and land. The Anthropocene recognizes that human activities have caused significant changes to the Earth's systems and caused climate change, deforestation, loss of biodiversity, pollution, and alteration of the carbon cycle.

The destruction of natural systems threatens the sustainability of life. This encompasses the effects on humanity that includes ourselves. We are currently witnessing the consequences not only in terms of environmental challenges but also social and economic ones.

The things we do to the natural system will come back to us like a boomerang and will affect our lives.

The upcoming generations deserve a better living environment that goes beyond just advanced technology for gaming and entertainment. While we have constructed impressive technologies, we have simultaneously destroyed the natural habitat that should have been a cherished companion, all in the name of progress.

In early childhood, the younger generation may enjoy technology and innovation. But as they grow older, they may come to resent it. They may feel that the previous generation stole their childhood with technology by taking away nature and peace of mind from them. The screen time of infants is increasing at an alarming rate to an extent where, some kids even become addicted to it before they turn one.

We are facing extreme weather conditions, pandemic situations, social anomalies, unpredictable market fluctuations, mass extinction of species and many other crises on Earth. This is the new normal.

Future generations will curse us for giving birth to them. They will also become the victims of the activities of their human ancestors. We messed up everything, which is irreversible and became a new normal.

The Food

"Foods that are dear to those in the mode of goodness
are those that are juicy, wholesome,
and pleasing to the heart.
These foods are said to increase the
duration of life, purify one's existence,
and give strength, health,
happiness, and satisfaction."
(Bhagavad Gita 17.8)

Once upon a time, there lived a king in a western kingdom. He had been experiencing frequent fever, cold episodes and stomach problems. In spite of seeking advice from numerous physicians and specialists, he was unable to find any relief for his ailments. It was during this time; the king's new chef was appraised for his creative cuisine. He decided to experiment with a tea recipe passed down to him from his Indian grandmother.

This tea was made using special ingredients like Pepper, Tulsi, and Cardamom, all of which were imported from India. The chef prepared the special medicated tea and served it to the king, who was hesitant at first but decided to try it anyway. As soon as he took the first sip, he felt a lightning sensation in his mouth and was pleasantly surprised by the taste. He felt much better after drinking the medicated tea. It seemed that his fever, stomach ache and cold have disappeared.

Overwhelmed with relief and gratitude, the king called the chef and praised him for his efforts. He even gifted the chef with some valuable items. However, the king was curious about the ingredients that had been used in the tea and he asked the chef to explain the recipe.

The chef told the king that his grandmother had taught him the recipe. The recipe included some important ingredients with pepper being the crucial one. Within a few days of continuous drinking of the medicated tea regularly, the king felt much healthier and energetic. This ignited a spark of interest in him to learn more about the key ingredients of this particular tea.

He was keenly impressed by the pepper and wanted to see the plant and meet the farmer who had cultivated it. He wanted to trace back the source of the pepper that he had consumed and felt a special connection. So, he decided to embark on a journey to India. Particularly to the state of Kerala, along with his ministers and officials. In order to search for the farmer who had grown the pepper.

The king finally located the farmer after searching for a long time. After connecting with many people and talking with several sellers and resellers, he planned to visit the farmer's house and pepper farm to praise him and to gift him. The king was dressed like an ordinary person so that nobody would realise that he was actually a king. When he reached the farmer's house and asked for the farmer who had planted the pepper plants, the farmer's son told him a heart-wrenching story.

The farmer had taken his own life by hanging himself on one of the pepper plants due to mounting debt. His family was planning to quit farming and leave the place. The king was shattered by this news and felt a deep sense of sorrow and responsibility. He realised that the pepper that he had consumed had come at a great cost and that he needed to help the farmer's family in some way.

He offered to help pay off the farmer's debts, and he promised to assist the family in any way that he could.

The king left the farmer's house, feeling a mix of emotions. On the one hand, he was grateful to have found the source of the Pepper that had helped cure his ailments, but on the other hand, he was saddened by the circumstances that had led to the farmer's death.

From that day on, the king always remembered the importance of the people behind the ingredients that he consumed and made a vow to know who is responsible for the food on the table and to support them in any way he could.

A dream about the suffering of farmers and the people behind how we get the food on our table made me think about knowing the people who convert soil into food by employing their knowledge, skills, and dedication. Their work involves managing soil health, nurturing crops, and making decisions to maximise agricultural productivity. Through their efforts; they ensure that we have a sustainable and reliable supply of food such as fruits, vegetables and other agricultural products. Despite their significant relevance to our lives which fails to acknowledge the numerous untold stories of suffering, love and the complexities of life.

Everyone should know who are the people responsible for the food we eat and we need to show gratitude to them at least in our thoughts when we are eating the food.

There are countless individuals who put in a tremendous amount of effort to ensure that we have food on our plates. That includes farmers who are unfortunately less valued, and unappreciated. They often struggle to make both ends meet. These hardworking individuals deserve much more than just financial compensation; they deserve our gratitude and respect for the invaluable service they provide.

Food Quality

As I walked along the streets on a weekend evening, my sights were set on finding a local market to purchase some fresh fish. It was difficult to know which ones were safe and which ones were not with so many vendors to choose from. But I have my special carry bag, a product with advanced technology. This bag was equipped with a sensor that could detect the presence of harmful chemicals such as formaldehyde which used to keep the fish fresh looking.

As I placed the fish into the bag, the sensor would activate and detect the fish for any contaminants. If any were detected, the bag would change its colour to indicate the presence of these chemicals and would warn me not to purchase the fish. This innovative carry bag was a true game-changer for anyone looking to buy fresh fish in a convenient and safe manner.

The sensor used in the bag was developed using the latest technology and could detect even the smallest amounts of contaminants. The bag's exterior was made of a special, flexible polymer that could change colour in response to the sensor's readings.

This was the dream. Having a carry bag that could tell me about the quality of the food products that I was buying. The idea that a bag could change colour to indicate the presence of contaminants in the food was a powerful motivator for me to work on the issue of contamination of fresh food products.

This dream made me feel a sense of urgency which is likely triggered by the widespread reports of formalin and other harmful chemicals being used to preserve fresh food such as fish in various parts of India. It was evident that a solution was needed to ensure the quality of the food we were consuming since numerous individuals were grappling with the issue of food adulteration and contamination.

So, I took this dream seriously and began to work on the problem of adulteration. It was a huge problem faced by almost everyone and many were not even aware of the quality of the food they were consuming. I felt that I had to do something to help solve this problem and bring awareness to the issue of food contamination.

During this time, I was in the process of planning my own venture and was considering various ideas for what to focus on. However, this dream of mine sparked a new idea in me; solving the problem of food adulteration.

I shared this dream with my friends, and we came to the conclusion that we should take action to address the issue of food fraud. The idea of a carry bag that could identify the quality of a product was intriguing, but we recognized that there would be many challenges to making it a reality.

While this approach of using a carry bag to identify the quality of a product is reactive, it would only solve the problem temporarily. We realised that in order to truly address the issue of adulteration, we needed to take a proactive approach that would address the root cause of the problem. We decided to investigate further and explore new and innovative solutions that could help to solve this issue on a more permanent basis.

As we delved deeper into the problem of food adulteration, it became clear that the traditional reactive approach of testing the food randomly after the problem occurs is similar to using a polythene bag to identify the quality of a product. It would not be enough to solve the problem at its root cause. The individuals who engage in food fraud would always find new ways to adulterate food for their own profit if the problem was not addressed at its core.

We discovered that many different types of food were being reported as adulterated, including cooking oil, milk, spice powders and almost all other types of food.

Through our research, we found that the major problem manufacturers faced was the unavailability of quality raw materials and the end consumer was not aware of the quality of the product they were buying. Most consumers only looked at the brand name and price before purchasing a product and did not have the time to learn about the food they were consuming.

As we reflected on this problem, we couldn't help but wonder if this was the negative impact of globalisation, capitalism, modernisation and industrialisation on our lives. We seemed to be running constantly towards something that would never truly satisfy us. In the process, we were forgetting about our health and our families. We were so focused on our targets for the month-end that we hardly had any time to think about anything else. This realisation made us more determined than ever to find a solution to the problem of food adulteration that would address its root cause and help consumers make informed decisions about the food they were consuming.

But when we neglect our health in the midst of our busy lives, we lose sight of the most important aspect of our existence. When people start adulterating food for profit, they are not only putting their own health at risk, but also making our entire species vulnerable to new diseases. The contamination of food may even lead to gene mutations.

In another dream of mine, there were stray dogs that consumed all the food waste. However, these dogs underwent mutations, resulting in a new generation of strays who lost their eyesight and were afflicted with various nervous disorders which led them to live in a state of perpetual suffering. Although this was merely a dream, it serves as a warning about the potential hazards of food adulteration and contamination.

Similarly, humans may suffer from mutations due to the increasing use of hormones, pesticides and other harmful chemicals in food preservation. We need to take a proactive approach to solving this problem at its root cause. The major cause of the problem was the unavailability of quality raw materials and a lack of transparency in quality. As people moved away from agriculture, the supply of quality raw materials decreased and it may take many decades to solve the problem of adulteration at its root level.

Our approach is to take a proactive approach to solving the problem of adulteration. We aim to ensure the traceability of products from farm to table, ensure the quality of the product in every batch and share the quality information transparently with the end consumer. This way we can ensure that the people are consuming safe and healthy food. Also helps in preserving our health and our environment.

As humans, we rely on food as our primary source of energy. This energy nourishes our body and mind, shaping our thoughts, words and actions. If we consume adulterated food, we introduce harmful energy into our bodies. This can manifest in the form of various diseases and unhealthy conditions.

It is crucial that we are aware of the contamination of heavy metals in our food. Heavy metal contamination is a significant issue in India and has been reported in many of our spice powders resulting in numerous cases of food poisoning in children. However, we often take these issues lightly until they affect someone close to us or ourselves. By then it will be too late and we will be left without hope.

Heavy metal contamination is often caused by intentional adulteration, such as the addition of colours, substandard ingredients or preservatives to increase a product's shelf-life or reduce its cost. It can also occur at the farming level, when farmland is located near an industrial area or when excessive amounts of chemical fertilisers or pesticides are used.

Children are particularly vulnerable to the effects of heavy metal contamination, especially if they are exposed to it while in the womb or during their early years. This exposure can lead to problems in the brain, internal organs, overall metabolism and can manifest in the form of disorders such as ADHD, memory loss and lack of focus. These issues can significantly impact a child's education and overall productivity in life. It is important to be mindful of the brand of food products we choose, as some may be contaminated with lead or other heavy metals that can have long-term detrimental effects on a child's development.

Consuming contaminated food with heavy metals, pesticides and hormones can have serious health consequences in children, including developmental delays, cognitive and behavioural problems, neurological damage and long-term health effects.

It is important to note that these effects may not always be immediately apparent, but can have long-term detrimental effects on the development and overall health of children. It is essential to take proactive measures to prevent food adulteration and protect the health of children and the entire population.

There have been several real-life cases of food adulteration and heavy metal contamination that have had serious health consequences for children. One example is the contamination of food with pesticides. In India, there have been many cases of pesticide residues found in food products, particularly fruits and vegetables. A study conducted in 2019 found that nearly 70% of fruits and vegetables samples tested in India had pesticide residue levels that exceeded the maximum limit set by the Food Safety and Standards Authority of India (FSSAI). This can cause health problems for children and adults, especially for children whose developing bodies and brains are more vulnerable to the toxic effects of pesticides.

There have been many cases of heavy metal contamination in foods as mentioned earlier. These include the presence of lead in spice powders, mercury in fish, cadmium in rice, and arsenic in drinking water. These incidents have led to food poisoning and even deaths in some cases.

These show that food adulteration and contamination with heavy metals is a serious issue that can have significant health consequences, particularly for children. It is essential that efforts are made to prevent and detect such adulteration and ensure that the food we consume is safe and healthy.

The food that we give to children during their early stages of growth is of utmost importance, as it can have long-term implications on their health and development. It is crucial that we carefully choose the food we provide to our children.

In India, there is a lack of proper diagnosis for food poisoning. Even if a child falls ill due to heavy metal poisoning, doctors may treat the disease. But without proper diagnosis, they may not know the underlying cause. This highlights the need for better diagnostic tools and awareness about food poisoning.

One way to ensure the quality of food for our children is by increasing awareness among parents about the food they purchase. The older generation would say that lack of knowledge is not a crime, but in today's world, not educating oneself about the food we consume is a criminal offence. Not only towards our children but also towards the future generations. We have access to resources that can help us gain knowledge about the food we consume and it is our responsibility to make use of these resources and educate ourselves about the food we purchase for our kids. Ignorance is not an excuse and we need to be vigilant about the food we feed our children. As it is key for their growth and development.

Make the world a better place

Making the world a better place is a complex and multifaceted challenge that requires thoughtful consideration out of limited resources. One approach to addressing this challenge is through an economic lens, where the goal is to invest resources in ways that can yield the greatest social returns.

Bjorn Lomborg, president of the Copenhagen Consensus Center has conducted extensive research with prominent economists to determine the best ways to invest resources to improve global welfare. In his book "How to Spend $75 Billion to Make the World a Better Place," Lomborg and his team analyse the United Nations Sustainable Development Goals and identify the areas where investments will have the greatest impact.

The research indicates that investing in global warming, education and child nutrition are among the top priorities. In particular, the team found that investing in child nutrition, especially during the first 1000 days of early childhood development offers the highest returns on investment. This is because providing essential nutrition and health support during this critical period can lead to improved brain capacity and immunity, which in turn can improve education and employability.

Note that child nutrition is not only crucial for the child's growth and development but also for building a resilient and healthy next generation which is able to face the challenges that come with the extreme conditions of climate change and new diseases. Investing in child nutrition is not only a moral duty but also a smart investment policy.

It is essential that we prioritise our investments and focus on areas where we can provide the greater good for the most people rather than feeling good about ourselves by investing in blue chip shares, stocks or in real estate. By investing in child nutrition, we can create a better future for all.

It is our societal responsibility to secure future generation's access to safe and nutritious food, considering the profound influence of climate change on food systems. Taking proactive measures now is vital to guarantee the availability of resources necessary for their well-being.

When starting a family, it is important to think about the kind of world we want to provide for our children. Providing them with healthy, authentic food is essential for their growth and development, and it is the basic responsibility of parents.

As individuals, we can make a commitment to educate ourselves about food and to make informed choices about what we eat. Eating a healthy diet can improve our health and help us live longer, but it is also important to think about the impact of our food choices on the environment and future generations.

Our startup team is dedicated to researching food and its effects on our bodies, and developing lifestyle modifications that promote health and longevity. We believe that by investing time and energy into understanding food and through promoting mindful eating, we can improve our health and the health of future generations.

We must also acknowledge that access to healthy food is not a given for everyone. By working together to improve food systems, we can ensure that everyone has access to nutritious food, regardless of their circumstances.

Education and awareness about quality food are crucial to achieving a healthy and sustainable world. As individuals, we have a responsibility to learn about the food we consume, it will impact on our health and the environment. This education should extend to the children in our care, as they are the future generation who will inherit the consequences of our food choices.

We must also take responsibility for ensuring that the food products we consume are ethically produced. This includes being mindful of where our food comes from, how it was produced, and the ingredients used. By supporting sustainable and ethical food practices, we can play a role in creating a more equitable and healthy food system. It is not only an ethical responsibility, but also a moral one, to ensure that our children are provided with quality food that will support their physical and mental well-being. Feeding them adulterated food is not only irresponsible but it can also have a detrimental effect on their health in the long run.

The Dance

In the infinite cosmos,
tiny strings, so subtle and small,
vibrates in the symphony of nothingness
Creating a dance, a formless cosmic arena.

From the tiniest atom to the grandest star,
The dance of vibrations had given them life.
the strings,the strands of existence,
Weaving together all that we ever knew.

The life, the death and the love
this dance that echoes through them.
We are the shadows of this cosmic romance.
In the eternal dance of strings.

"If you want to know the secret of the universe, think in terms of Energy, Frequency and Vibration."

- Nikola Tesla

As we delve deeper into the quantum realm of matter, such as molecules, atoms, neutrons and quarks; we discover that they are composed of very tiny strings vibrating at different frequencies and patterns. These vibrations give rise to different particles, which in turn contribute to the vastness and diversity of our universe.

String theory, a widely known concept in modern quantum physics, is both fascinating and perplexing. It is an attempt to unify the various forces of the universe and realise Einstein's dream of a unified theory of physics.

Why are things the way they are in our universe? Our world would be odd and deadly if any of its underlying rules were even slightly different. Rather, it appears to be finely tuned to make life possible. Possibly, string theory can explain the reason.

According to string theory, we live in a multiverse, which means there could be millions of universes with different natural constants and even different laws of physics. Many physicists believe this is a contradiction in the theory but scientists believe it may actually help us understand why our universe is able to sustain life.

Despite its potential to explain the mysteries of the universe, string theory has faced criticism due to its untestable nature. However, some scientists argue that it may be able to shed light on why our universe is so fine-tuned for life. They suggest that after the Big Bang, the universe was governed by a single force, which later divided into the four fundamental forces we know today: strong force, weak force, electromagnetic force and gravitational force.

String theory proposes the existence of 11 dimensions, including 10 spatial dimensions and 1 dimension of time. It also suggests that our universe is one among an infinite number of multiverses, each with its own set of natural constants and laws of physics.

String theory is a difficult concept to test and it has yet to be proven, but it holds the potential to solve some of the universe's deepest mysteries. Many scientists are searching for theories that can explain the existence of our reality and string theory may be able to assist in this quest.

According to this theory, these vibrating strings are the fundamental fabric of the cosmos and all we see is a collection of dancing strings when viewed at a subatomic level. The universe appears to be a non-dual entity.

In string theory, the concept of non-duality refers to the idea that the universe is a single entity made up of vibrating strings. So that all the different particles and forces in the universe are simply various manifestations of these strings and that the universe can be thought of as a single, non-dual entity. This idea is in contrast to the traditional duality of classical physics, which views the universe as made up of separate and distinct objects that interact through forces.

The beauty and depth of the theory changed my perspective of myself and the world around me and I was excited about the possibilities it presents. At the subatomic level, there is no distinction between living and non-living things; perhaps the only difference is a slight variation in the frequency of a cluster of strings.

The nature of reality becomes particularly fascinating at the quantum level. The behaviour of particles and systems is described by probability distributions rather than definite, predictable outcomes. This inherent uncertainty gives rise to phenomena such as superposition and entanglement, where particles can exist in multiple states simultaneously or become instantaneously connected regardless of distance.

In this quantum realm, the traditional boundaries and discriminations that we observe in the macroscopic world seem to break down. Anything becomes possible and particles can exhibit contradictory properties at the same time. However, when we change our observation from the quantum level to the macroscopic scale, these potentialities collapse and everything seems to be concrete and in definite states, leading to the world we perceive as real. This duality between the quantum realm and the three-dimensional world presents a profound philosophical question about the nature of reality. What is truly "real"?

I was confused about what the "real" was, as anything is possible at the quantum level, but not all of those things are possible in our three-dimensional world of reality. This dual experience of non-duality is the weirdest part. The major change in my mind was the realisation of our insignificance in the grand scheme of things and that we are simply a result of strings that we did not create.

Our existence and the characteristics of the surrounding world are shaped by the interplay of these strings. We are interconnected with the fabric of reality, and that is influenced by countless factors which lie beyond our individual control. When we attempt to understand our own existence, it appears as though the strings and particles are striving to comprehend themselves by taking the form of a human.

We accumulate various objects throughout our lives, attributing meaning and value to them and these possessions are often seen as symbols of success, status, and security. However, when we delve deeper into the nature of ownership and possessions, we begin to realise that their significance is ultimately illusory and the possessions and claims are insignificant. Fixing one's actions and existence entirely upon this misconception of accumulating possessions and ownership is merely foolishness. The accumulation of possessions in our lives is a reflection of societal conditioning and our own attachment to external forms.

Even our physical bodies that we often perceive as the ultimate form of personal possession, are not truly independent entities. Our bodies are composed of atoms and particles that have existed for billions of years, continuously changing their forms and shapes. The air we breathe, the food we eat and the water we drink are all part of a web of interconnectedness which sustains our existence. We are not isolated beings but rather entangled with the environment, other living beings and the cosmos.

Recognizing the delusion of independent ownership can lead to a shift in perspective. Instead of clinging to possessions as a source of identity and security, we can cultivate a greater sense of gratitude and appreciation for the interconnectedness and synchronicity of all things. By letting go of the delusion of ownership, we can embrace a more profound understanding of our interconnected existence and find true fulfilment in the intangible aspects of life.

We can experience the feeling of aliveness as a unique and personal sensation. The feeling of aliveness is often associated with a heightened sense of being present, engaged, and aware of our own existence. It includes a sense of vitality, energy and connection to the world around us. It may arise during moments of intense joy, excitement, or passion when a person feels fully alive and in tune with their surroundings. The feeling of aliveness can be a deeply personal and subjective experience and it is indeed a sensation that we as individuals can possess.

The feeling of aliveness is an indescribable phenomenon, and we should consider ourselves lucky to experience it for a limited period of time, apparently our lifespan. Perhaps these tiny strings and fundamental forces of the cosmos had to combine in a certain way to take our shape and form and to become aware of their own existence. All these searches and queries about ourselves are like consciousness trying to understand itself.

The concept of the dual experience within non-duality can be seen as a playful irony within the universe. It seems that the universe, in all its complexity, forms intricate patterns and shapes, including the phenomenon of life and the various emotions and situations that comes with it, such as anger, sadness, jealousy and vengeance. From a certain perspective, it can be amusing to consider how seriously we often take these formations, as if they hold supreme importance.

As to the purpose behind this playful puppetry, it is difficult to ascertain a definite answer. The nature of existence and consciousness remains a profound mystery. It could be a revelation that this cosmic dance serves no particular purpose at all and is simply the unfolding of mystery behind existence itself. Or perhaps there is some deeper meaning or lesson to be discovered through our experiences and interactions.

From my sincere and serious efforts to understand theories of quantum mechanics, I realised that these strings were simply having fun, just dancing as they pleased. But we, the same consciousness in a cluster, form and shape, worry about things like hair loss, skin colour, financial obligations and an extensive array of matters that weigh heavily on our minds.

So, if you are reading this you need to understand that you are simply lucky. You have a shape and form to understand this consciousness and you are educated enough to read and understand this. We are nothing more than a collection of energy strings, having fun and experiencing the universe through our shape and form. By realising that we are nothing more than a feeling, we can let go of our fears and worries about losing something that we never truly owned. We are simply the consciousness itself, experiencing the world around us.

Even death is just a change in the vibration of certain energy strings at a certain frequency. But nothing truly goes away, as everything belongs to the same conscious being. Nothing truly disappears because everything is interconnected within a singular conscious entity. Whether we are alive or deceased, intelligent or not, affluent or impoverished, peaceful or violent, virtuous or malevolent, we all belong to this unified whole. The profound connection encompasses all entities, including ourselves, the very book you are reading and even the grains of sand beneath us.

This realisation should inspire us to recognize that we are all interconnected, forming a singular conscious being. The diversity and apparent separation we perceive are merely manifestations of the real magic of the consciousness.

String theory has the potential to change one's perspective on life and the cosmos. Even though it has yet to be proven, the beauty of the concept can be life-changing for some individuals. During one of the toughest times in my life, filled with heartbreak, despair, and depression, stumbling upon Brian Greene's presentation on string theory completely changed how I perceived the world around me. The sheer elegance and wonder of the concept infused new life into me thus instilled a renewed sense of hope

I wholeheartedly urge those who are seeking motivation and a sense of clarity in their lives to delve deep into the captivating realm of quantum physics and science. Embrace the incredible power of science as a tool to unravel the mysteries of our own existence and the enchanting world around us. It has the potential to ignite a spark of wonder, unlocking new perspectives that can uplift and inspire us on our journey of self-discovery. Give yourself the gift of exploring the awe-inspiring wonders of reality and let its captivating beauty guide you towards a deeper understanding of yourself and the remarkable tapestry of existence.

The process of learning can be compared to the metamorphosis of a caterpillar into a butterfly. In much the same way that a caterpillar feasts on leaves and enters a profound slumber, called pupa, before emerging as a resplendent butterfly, we embark on our own learning voyage by establishing a steadfast groundwork in the realm of science. This profound understanding allows us to grasp the very essence of reality and sets us on a remarkable path of discovery and growth.

Once we have acquired wisdom from external sources such as books and the internet, we possess the remarkable ability to embark on an introspective journey, delving into a profound meditative state that enables us to connect with the true essence of reality from within. This transformative internal process can be likened to the emergence of a butterfly, symbolising our innate potential to spread our wings and soar freely. In this sacred space of inner awakening, we shed the layers of illusion and embrace our authentic selves. We transcend the limitations imposed by societal conditioning and evolve into the boundless potential that resides within us. They will be wiser and kind who break the moral conditioning of society. Like the butterfly soaring through the open sky, we find liberation in embracing our true nature, free from doubts or fears.

Science as a Tool

Science took humanity from the invention of the steam engine to the creation of the nuclear bomb. But we must not forget the ethical considerations that come with utilising science as a tool. It is a challenging choice to make but a layer of ethics should be there above the decision to use any tool. Science is a great tool but what choices we make with them is the real challenge.

There is no doubt that medical science has made significant advancements in engineering and technology, allowing for ground-breaking procedures such as heart transplants.

For e.g: Precision Medicine: Precision medicine involves tailoring medical treatment and interventions based on an individual's unique genetic makeup, environment and lifestyle. This approach has transformed the management of various diseases, including cancer by enabling targeted therapies and personalised treatment plans.

Artificial Heart: Scientists and researchers have developed artificial heart devices that can temporarily replace the function of a failing heart while awaiting a heart transplant. These devices, such as the Total Artificial Heart (TAH), mimic the pumping action of a natural heart and can keep patients alive until a suitable donor's heart gets available.

However, despite these advancements, a significant number of people around the world continue to suffer from dietary-based diseases such as; heart disease and diabetes which claims more lives.

It would be beneficial for science to focus on educating the public about these diseases and preventive measures rather than solely focusing on developing advanced medicines to treat them. One reason for this motive is, many dietary-based disorders could be prevented or managed through lifestyle changes and better education. However, it is also important to note that there are often financial incentives for the development of new medicines, as they can be a profitable venture for companies. This raises ethical concerns about whether the focus on profit-making is overshadowing the pursuit of scientific knowledge and the betterment of human health.

It is crucial to remember that while scientific advancements can bring positive benefits, they can also have negative consequences if not used responsibly. It is important to consider the ethical implications of scientific research such as ensuring the welfare and rights of human subjects, the responsible treatment of animals in research, protecting data privacy and security, managing the dual-use potential of technologies, minimising environmental impact, promoting equity and fairness, upholding intellectual property and publication ethics and considering global perspectives. Adhering to ethical guidelines and fostering collaboration between researchers, policymakers and society, helps to ensure that scientific progress is pursued responsibly for the greater good.

Science offers hope for addressing issues such as extreme climate change and pandemics, but the ethical considerations of how to use this knowledge and technology can be challenging. However, in the context of scientific advancements and developments, we often see greed, ego and a lack of good intentions guiding decision making. It is important to remember that while science can bring many benefits, it is crucial to approach it with a sense of ethics and responsibility and to consider the long-term consequences of our choices.

Free Will

We are often led to believe that we have complete control over our lives and the choices we make, but in reality, many aspects of our existence are predetermined by forces beyond our control. Our families, gender, vulnerabilities and our names are also chosen for us by the universe. Even the most important aspects of our lives, such as our experiences and the events that shape us are not necessarily within our power to choose.

This realisation can be difficult to accept, as it calls into question our sense of agency and free will. However, it is important to remember that just because certain things are predetermined, it does not mean that we are incapable of making meaningful choices. Our ability to make decisions, even small ones, such as choosing what to eat or what to wear, is still important and valuable.

Quantum mechanics and neuroscience have revealed that the notion of free will is illusory. Our choices are intricately influenced by a complex interplay of genetics, environment, and past experiences. This realisation doesn't diminish the importance of our choices, but rather highlights the multitude of factors that shape our decisions. While certain aspects of our existence may be predetermined, we still retain the ability to exercise choice and actively mould our own experiences. It is essential to grasp the intricate nature of free will and acknowledge the constraints on our agency in order to navigate life's complexities more effectively.

Free will exists when we see chocolate in a store and we wish to eat it, then we purchase and consume it. Enjoying that chocolate is a kind of free will, but that freewill or rather ability to make things happen according to our will, won't be there in the case of flipping a dice and one cannot choose the result with the toss. We may make possible options of the toss using the dice odds, but we cannot determine or decide the outcome. In short, one cannot meddle with the idea of probability.

When you believe you have made a choice, but the concept of "you" is not separate from the larger conscious field. Both you and I are interconnected parts of this conscious field, where particles exist and shape our bodies, brains, and the experiences we undergo. It is possible that the experiences we perceive are chosen by the conscious field, which communicates with the brain and selects the experiences we believe we have chosen.

The idea of a conscious field has been contemplated by philosophers and scientists for centuries, but a definitive explanation of what this field is, and how it operates remains elusive. Nonetheless, several theories have been proposed regarding this.

One theory proposes that the conscious field is an energy field that pervades existence. This field comprises tiny particles of consciousness which interact with each other to generate our experiences. Consequently, our experiences influence the development and functioning of our brains.

Another theory suggests that the conscious field is an information field. This field contains information about everything that has transpired till now or will transpire in future. The conscious field is in constant flux. When we have experiences, we tap into this information. Then, our experiences shape the way we interpret and perceive this information.

The idea suggests that the conscious field has two aspects in which, the first aspect is, operating as an energy field and the later aspect consists of functioning as an information field that shapes our experiences. The energy field forms the foundation of consciousness, while the information field brings our experiences into life by giving them different shapes and characteristics.

If consciousness comprises both an energy field and an information field, it implies that consciousness has both physical and non-physical aspects. The energy field would constitute the physical foundation of consciousness, enabling basic functions such as perception and decision-making. The information field, on the other hand, would facilitate more intricate aspects of consciousness, such as thinking, experiencing emotions, and spiritual encounters.

Whether the conscious field is primarily an energy field, an information field or a combination of both, it is evident that it occupies a central role in our lives. We can perceive ourselves as clusters of interconnected energy and information fields, momentarily distinguished by a thin layer of separation. This interconnection shapes and forms our bodies and experiences. But ultimately, we are all interconnected and part of a greater supreme being.

So, we are not separate from the conscious field to have a distinctive experience of our own.

Theoretical physicist Brian Greene suggests that every individual is essentially composed of particles and is subject to the principles of physics. Consequently, any action we undertake can be attributed to the movements and interactions of these particles within our bodies. He said that, when he writes a book or solves a complex physics equation, he acknowledges that it is ultimately due to the coordinated efforts of particles and the various forces at play in the shape of Brain Greene which resulted in the desired outcome of compelling a book or solving the equation. This is a better approach rather than taking credit alone for doing something.

From the neuroscience perspective, the decisions we make are already decided by the brain even before we intend to make them. The brain is making the choice mechanically, not with our conscious decision. But we feel an illusion about making the decision.

Benjamin Libet, a pioneering scientist in human consciousness, conducted an experiment on the existence of free will. In Libet's experiment, participants were asked to sit in front of a timer and were requested to perform a simple task such as clicking a button or flexing their wrist. They were asked to report the moment when they become consciously aware of the decision to move, while EEG electrodes on their heads tracked their brain function.

Libet repeatedly demonstrated that unconscious brain activation was correlated with the movement for an average of half a second. Before the participants become aware of the decision to move, a transition in EEG impulses which Libet named as; "readiness potential" happens.

The participants did not realise they had decided to move until half a second after the movement had already begun. This finding supports the idea that the brain initiates actions before we are consciously aware of them. The delay between the brain's decision and our conscious awareness creates an opportunity for us to attribute our actions to our own intentions.

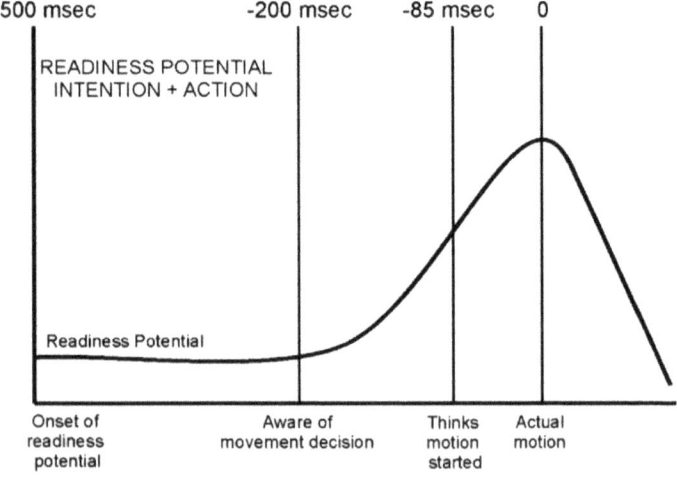

(Fig: 1) (Image courtesy: The neuroscientific foundations of free will, Zvi Harry Rappaport)

The above diagram illustrates the result of the Libet experiment where the brain's choice of making the decision even before we consciously think we made the decision.

According to Quantum Mechanics and Neuroscience, the concept of free will is questioned, suggesting that it might be an illusion. Quantum Mechanics proposes that the behaviour of particles and events in the universe is governed by probabilities rather than determinism. Potentially implying that our actions are influenced by unpredictable quantum events. Neuroscience experiments, which includes Benjamin Libet's research, provide evidence that the brain's activity associated with an action takes place prior to our conscious awareness of deciding to carry out that action. This suggests that our sense of free will could be a retrospective interpretation of events, with our brain activity shaping our actions subconsciously. Which followed by our conscious experience of making a choice.

The realisation that free will may be an illusion can sometimes lead to fatalistic thoughts and a sense of being exempt from accountability for our actions. However, as humans, we are accountable for our actions and behaviours.

Even if free will is ultimately an illusion, we experience the perception of making choices in our daily lives. We still have the capacity to compare options, consider consequences, and act based on our intentions and desires. Within the frameworks of society and ethics, we are held accountable for the outcomes of our actions.

We owe our gratitude to the process of evolution for granting humans a highly developed prefrontal cortex, which provides us with increased self-control. This cognitive ability allows us to manage emotions, make decisions and maintain discipline. With the prefrontal cortex, we can take responsibility for our actions, align them with our values, and be accountable for their consequences. Embracing this responsibility fosters personal growth and encourages an ethical and conscientious approach to our behaviours.

While external factors and unconscious processes can influence our decision-making, we possess the ability to reflect, learn and adapt. We can analyse our actions, take responsibility for mistakes and strive to make improvements. It is true that we cannot control the outside world or determine the events that occur in our lives. However, we do have the power to cultivate discipline and prepare ourselves to navigate new situations. The only option we truly have is to develop personal discipline and readiness in order to face the challenges that life presents.

We often operate with limited knowledge, relying on our ability to make guesses, assumptions and consider various possibilities about events in our daily lives. The key to success lies in our capacity to selectively focus on the information that is most relevant and discard irrelevant information. This process involves identifying and retaining meaningful information that aids us in achieving our goals. If we rely on religious belief systems rather than the progression of scientific research to acquire knowledge, there may come a time when our survival is challenged. If we lack the necessary information, skills and knowledge to ensure our survival, as a species, we could face the risk of extinction.

When it comes to acquiring knowledge, there are two types: learning from personal experiences and learning from the experiences of others. Learning from personal experiences can be time-consuming and demanding, requiring significant effort could be called hard work. On the other hand, learning from others' experiences is often seen as a more efficient approach, requiring less time and energy. It is often referred to as smart work.

We should prioritise seeking satisfaction within ourselves rather than relying solely on external sources, as our ability to find it may be limited by the lack of free will. Instead, it is important to focus on self-reflection and inner listening. Rather than being solely goal-oriented, we should adopt a growth-oriented mindset. By prioritising personal growth, we enhance our experiences and find happiness in the knowledge that we have progressed from our previous selves. It is through this ongoing process of growth that we can find true fulfilment.

When we strive for a goal, we often assess the disparity between our current mindset and the desired future. During this evaluation, we envision ourselves as happy and fulfilled in the future, but not in the present. Consequently, we tend to criticise ourselves for our perceived weaknesses and believe that we must address them in order to achieve our goals. This self-judgement can cause us to underrate the essence of the journey we are undertaking. We think ourselves inferior and incomplete at this very moment and this feeling never makes us happy. We forget the present moment, the here and now, which is what keeps us away from happiness. We should be happy now, for whatever we are. If we are not, we will never be.

Instead of trying to improve on something you are weak in, allow yourself to grow. This can be achieved by taking care of our health through the consumption of quality food, nurturing our peace of mind by seeking out high-quality information and cultivating our skills through disciplined practice and engaging in a variety of experiences. When we talk about developing skills, it is important to pursue activities that we genuinely enjoy and are passionate about. Discipline can be cultivated in various aspects of our lives, starting from our thoughts, words and actions. In Indian knowledge systems there is a concept of discipline in breathing techniques, where the aim is to train and discipline ourselves. By adopting these principles, we can foster holistic growth and development.

The Bhagavad Gita primarily focuses on guiding individuals to make appropriate decisions in various situations. Krishna imparts wisdom to Arjuna, emphasising the significance of detached attachment in carrying out one's countless responsibilities. He introduces the notion of "choicelessness," which denotes a state where individuals act without being emotionally tied to the consequences of their actions. This means that a person should do their duty or perform their actions without any desire or expectation of a particular result.

In other words, a person should act without any personal preferences, bias, or attachment to the outcome and instead focus on the action itself.

Krishna explains that the universe is governed by a cosmic law and every action has its consequences. Therefore, one must perform their actions with a sense of duty and responsibility, without being influenced by personal desires or attachments. One should play their role in this cosmic drama without judging or taking everything personally; merely perceive life as a play. When he said that, he implied that the whole array of events cannot be chosen by us. Instead, let those experiences which need us choose us.

Krishna was called a complete man because of this approach. He was like a good musician; he never chose a path; the path chose him. This means he never stuck to only one way. If another way opened to him, he always took that opportunity. He even said that nothing is absolutely right or wrong; it is all in our mind. If you think something is right for you, you can do it, because there is nothing 'fundamentally serious' here! We tend to take everything too personally and we get doubts about whether we are getting it right or wrong, which may lead to a dilemma.

Krishna's idea of choicelessness also encompasses the understanding that promises and plans made by individuals are subject to change according to the greater plan of the consciousness. For example, before the Kurukshetra war began, Krishna made a promise not to wield any weapons in the battle.

This decision was seen as a demonstration of his neutrality and his commitment to guiding Arjuna without directly participating in the war.

But, during the battle, Krishna noticed that Bhishma was fighting with unmatched valour and skill, causing heavy losses to the Pandava forces. He was also a devotee of Krishna, and he knew that Krishna would not kill him. So, Bhishma challenged Krishna to break his vow, knowing that Krishna would not be able to resist. Krishna was indeed infuriated, and he picked up a wheel from a chariot and threw it at Bhishma and he fell to the ground. He then told Arjuna that he had broken his vow in order to achieve a greater outcome. This illustrates that even the best-laid plans can be altered by the need of the hour and situation and that individuals should be open to change and adapt to the circumstances that arise.

The belief that individuals have free will and control over their reality is an illusion created by the ego. In reality, we are not in control of the events that happen in our lives, and it is important to let go of this illusion in order to align ourselves with the will of the consciousness itself. Instead of trying to control our reality, we should focus on listening to ourselves and developing the discipline to better deal with external events.

By observing our thoughts without judgement and releasing our attachment to our ego, we can cultivate a more peaceful and fulfilling state of mind. This is because when we are able to see our thoughts for what they are, rather than identifying with them, we are able to free ourselves from the negative emotions that they often generate. We can then align ourselves with the will of the consciousness, which is the universal source of love, peace, and joy.

Fire and Flame

The whole existence is like fire and flames. From a narrow perspective, we can only see the flames. But from a wider perspective, we see fire. When our attention is solely on individual flames, they might appear separate and distinct, but broadening our perspective reveals their interconnectedness as integral components of a shared underlying reality.

We all are different flames of the same fire. Me, You and all things around us are in the same fire or single entity.

We can see different shapes of flames on the fire and flames spontaneously ignite and destroy themselves along with changing their shapes. but the whole fire matters, not a single flame. The relevance of the flame may be significantly less when we see it from a wider angle and what matters is fire.

Even when we think from the perspective of a flame, the flame doesn't have free will or rather it can't control the fire. Even if some flames believe it has control over the fire, it is lame. If any part of the flame thinks that it can claim the fire, it misses the whole point. They may become the momentary masters of fire; but ultimately, they are just part of the fire.

The flame doesn't have possessions. Existence of the flame is random in the process of fire, but is important too.

In Bhagavad Gita, Krishna encourages us to surrender to the conscious will and perform our duties in a life without attachment to the outcome. Life is a play or drama, and we are all actors on the stage as Shakespeare rightly pointed out. Our experiences, emotions, and actions are all part of the drama and we should learn to play our roles without becoming too attached or too affected by them.

The contact between the senses and the sense objects gives rise to sensations of hot and cold, pleasure and pain which are temporary and fleeting. These experiences come and go like the seasons. Therefore, you should learn to tolerate them without being disturbed.

The problem starts when the flame thinks on its own and they start formulating theories about themselves and fire being unaware of the whole thing.

In a world where everyone is vying for power, equality is often used as a false promise. Some offer equality in order to gain control over others. While some people believe that it is the right thing to do. This is a common tactic used by many people throughout history. Unfortunately, it often leads to more division and inequality rather than equality in its true form and sense. However, Absolute equality is not possible in reality and it is not even necessarily desirable.

A better thing we already have from existence is oneness; this idea suggests that everything in existence is interconnected, and there is no separation between things. Instead of striving for equality, we should recognize our interconnectedness and work towards harmonious coexistence.

The recognition of our inherent interconnectedness may lead to a profound shift in how we view ourselves and our relationship with others. We start to see that the things we do, the choices we make and the way we treat others have an impact on the world around us.

One of the most significant ways in which this shift can manifest is in how we approach the issue of inequality. When we realise that we are all part of the same web of life, it becomes harder to justify treating some people as lesser than others. We start to see that the well-being of one person is intimately connected to the well-being of others also.

At the quantum level, science has shown that we are all interconnected and share a common plane of reality. Given this oneness, it may seem futile to engage in conflict over things that are not inherent to our nature. We are all one after all. Then why bother demanding and struggling for things that are already present?

Achieving oneness does not require any physical fights or bloodshed, but it does require a fundamental shift in our mindset and a deep understanding of our interconnectedness.

Realising oneness is indeed a difficult task because it requires a significant change in how we perceive ourselves and the world around us. Accepting this interconnectedness can be difficult. Because we are all conflict-loving people, we don't like peace. We humans have a tendency to enjoy conflicts rather than peace. We like to find things that provoke fights and make us feel victorious, as it aligns with our strong beliefs and values. We are conditioned to thrive on conflict, seeking out opportunities to engage in heated debates and arguments, often at the expense of creating harmony and understanding.

We have inherited the conditioning to seek out problems, embrace diversity and engage in conflicts. All of it stems from our past. Darwin's theory proposed the concept of "survival of the fittest," implied that we must compete and clash in order to survive. However, this is an outdated notion. The true and contemporary approach is to foster collaboration rather than conflict and to engage in co-creation instead of competition. Throughout nature, collaboration and co-creation have always been instrumental in generating new possibilities.

We are taught to measure success by how much we have achieved individually rather than how much we have contributed to the greater good.

Collaboration and co-creation are essential for the future because they promote cooperation and mutual understanding among individuals, groups, and organisations. It allows for the exchange of ideas and perspectives, leading to more efficient problem-solving and the development of new and innovative solutions.

There are many reasons why we need to collaborate and co-create instead of engaging in conflict and competition.

Collaboration and co-creation bring various benefits, including innovation, increased efficiency, enhanced creativity, greater flexibility, better decision making, improved relationships, greater empowerment, better adaptability, increased resilience and greater scalability. By working together, individuals and groups can achieve more than they would on their own and generate sustainable solutions.

The Tree

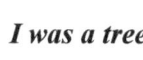

I was a tree
For ages.
Fruiting, sprouting, and
shedding the leaves with seasons.

Leaning, tilting
My shade spread far and wide
Squirrels nested in my branches
Migratory birds feasted on my fruits

I stood firmly rooted in mother earth
The sun gave me light like a father
Nothing but bliss

As a tree, I dreamed of being a man
To roam free and explore all I can.
I Wished to relinquish my tree form
And be reborn as a human being
For at least one life.

Arjun Freeman

Born as a human being
Through the magic of nature.
I laughed without joy
I cried without sadness
Tired of lying
Devastating and destroying nature
Without bliss.
I found solace in the drunkenness of alcohol.

Once again, I wish to be a seed
and fall onto the ground and sprout.
Grow as a plant
Then a tree, a giant tree
Shedding leaves with the seasons
Sprouting and fruiting with the hope
To spread my shade once more.

There was a treasure hunter who was in search of the most precious stones and treasures. He had dedicated his life to finding the most valuable crystal in the world. He searched all his life. In the meantime, he collected many treasures. But those collections could not satisfy him.

He explored the seas, walked through forests, mountains and very dangerous remote locations where even light may not reach the ground. He dedicated his whole life to finding the most precious stone, so much so that he spent very little time in his own home.

On his mission to find the most precious crystal, he found himself walking through a dense forest. He walked through that forest for weeks and satiated his hunger with some fruits and leaves he collected on the way.

Finally, he entered a deep cave. As he moved deeper into the cave, it became darker and he saw a box on a rock in the fading light of his torch when he had almost reached the end. He somehow managed to open it. He was stunned to see the light emitted out of the box, and he could make out the words written inside the cover of the box: "The treasure was inside you all along." When he read that, he became confused. Even though he attempted to look inside the box, he could not see anything clearly because the light from the box was too bright and blinding, much like gazing directly into the blinding brilliance of the sun. In his excitement to see inside the box, he leaned towards it. But he suddenly felt dizzy, and he could feel that his hands and legs were shivering. Somehow, he managed to put his hands inside the box to touch the bottom. But the whole box gulped him suddenly. He fell into the light inside the box. He felt himself being pulled towards the bottom of the box. Just as a black hole grab anything that comes near it, he feels himself being pulled deeper into the box and unable to escape. He was in ecstasy and forgot himself, even the fact that he was being absorbed into the crystal. But suddenly, he felt as if he was falling into a sea, falling to the surface like a meteor burning up in the atmosphere and vanishing on the horizon. A whole new world of reality opened to him.

The crystal was a portal to another world and in this new world, he was no longer a human, but a seed of a tree. The seed fell to the ground and gradually grew into a giant, expansive tree that provided shelter and nourishment to countless life forms. The mind and soul of the treasure hunter was now inside the tree, experiencing the highest levels of bliss and joy. He felt like he had finally reached the state of mind he had always desired.

This dream made me think about the nature of a tree. How wonderful it must be to be a tree, always in bliss, in its own way. The tree probably never had an enemy and all the animals and birds around it spread love. Many animals depend on it for survival, and when the tree needs food, mother nature always provides. The tree never complains. When the season changes, it sheds leaves, grows new leaves, flowers and keeps going on.

The tree is the best role model you can follow; be like a tree, with zero ego, no enemies, and full of love. It is always full of life, stands firmly on the ground, and mother nature feeds the tree with all the love it holds. The sun provides all the energy, and the spring, winter, summer, autumn, and rainy seasons bring new experiences to it. Even in all seasons, it stands blissful in its own deep state of consciousness. Many times, I have felt that trees are the highest level of consciousness.

To become a tree is very easy; one must have zero ego. The tree has no ego at all and it always grows more and more every day within nature. Ego is something we need to manage in our life to become blissful like a tree.

Ego is the only thing that we possess; the rest are owned by nature itself, or by the conscious field, our body, our mind, our soul, or whatever we have. But ego is our creation. Ego is our self-possessed imagination, an illusion that we have created for ourselves. We did not create our body and we cannot own it. We do not own anything we think we have and it is all part of nature and this conscious field. We own only our ego, the feeling of being separate from this field. Ego is what we grow in the mind. It is the self-image we create about ourselves that is almost fake, but we nevertheless create an image about ourselves to keep things moving. Ego is the leading figure and the villain. It is how we describe ourselves, our name, community, all the identity makers and tags from our childhood which we carry in front of the world. Ego shapes not only ourselves but also the energy around us. It is a cage we created that imprison us.

Ego is a self-created illusionary circle of identity that arises from attachment to external factors, such as possessions, achievements, and social status. It distorts our perception, creating a false sense of self-importance and separateness from others. It hinders one from accessing their true being and prevents freedom and self-awareness.

By stepping outside our ego, we gain a clearer perspective on reality through questioning our beliefs and biases. Simultaneously, stepping inside ourselves through introspection, allows us to explore our authentic selves and align our actions with our true values. When we picture ego, it is the image we compare with someone else, where we may see ourselves as either bigger or smaller in comparison. However, this comparison obscures the understanding of our true selves and it becomes dangerous when ego starts dictating our choices.

By shedding the illusions of ego, we can embrace authenticity, compassion and deeper connections with ourselves and others. By recognizing the dangers of ego and actively choosing to transcend it, we reclaim the power to make choices aligned with our authentic being.

When you have a dream; which you see from your childhood might have formed in your mind without your conscious thought process. It is a natural expression of your being since you are an integral part of nature. Your dreams are born within you, reflecting your innate desires and aspirations. Following your dreams is thus an organic and instinctive way of determining what to do with your life.

But when you don't work towards your dream and instead choose something that your ego suggests to keep up the image in society that your ego demands, it is unnatural and may never satisfy your mind. To satisfy your ego, you choose something you don't wish to do. But you will always blame your choices for your life and you cannot be happy.

But when you follow your dreams, it is natural. That choice is made by nature. When you don't follow your dreams and spend your life on something else, which your ego chooses, it is not natural. When your inferiority or superiority complex chooses your path, and when you don't follow your dreams and follow something else, it results in a loss for yourself and society.

Even when you follow your dream, it might not be easy to reach the desired destination. You need to become a man of no ego to follow that dream. So, there are many situations which you need to go through to manifest that dream. However, it is crucial to persevere and remain committed as this is how you liberate yourself from the clutches of ego.

The whole system will test your strength and capacity to reach that level. But when you don't quit and still move ahead further without any ego, you will be rewarded with what you wished for. But the truth is, you are not achieving anything; you allow nature to flow through you without blocking the flow with ego.

The Surrender

2020 has held immense promises and anticipations for many people across the globe. Dreams and aspirations had been building up for a long time, with the new decade viewed as a fresh beginning full of potential by everyone. However, these hopes were abruptly shattered by the devastating emergence of COVID-19. The impact of the pandemic left me feeling deeply frustrated, irritated, and even depressed.

Personally, I was disheartened because I had just embarked on my entrepreneurial journey with the establishment of my start-up in 2018. The year 2020 was supposed to be a pivotal moment for its growth and success. However, the pandemic threw a wrench into those plans, dashing the hopes and expectations I had nurtured for my venture.

The anger made me hate everything imaginable. I started hating the people around me, the government, the corporations, and even if there is a supreme being, I hated it more than anything. I expressed my frustration by scolding it in very disrespectful language. I was angry about the situation I was in and continuously scolded the superconscious being throughout my day because I was so furious with the situation.

One day, I was working in my workspace when I suddenly felt something get stuck under the toes of my right leg. At first, I didn't pay much attention to it, but as time passed, the pain in my leg started to intensify. Eventually, I decided to go back home and examine the cause of the pain.

To my surprise, I saw what appeared to be a black needle embedded in my skin. There were no visible wounds where the splinter had entered. Intrigued, I took a blade and carefully cut the outer layer of skin, revealing a thin black wire-like object. As I pulled it out, I felt a shock. It turned out to be a strand of hair that had somehow grown inside my skin, underneath my toes.

Curiosity got the better of me, and I wanted to make sure if this was a normal occurrence or a sign of a more complicated health issue. So, I turned to Google for answers. After a while, I came across a term called "hair splinter." I learned that while it is a rare incident, it is considered normal in terms of health. It may happen to individuals who deal with a lot of hair, such as barbers or professionals involved in pet hair grooming.

What struck me as odd was that, I wasn't involved in any hair-related job or work. However, I realised that I used to utter disrespectful words about the supreme being in my regional language. Specifically, I would scold the supreme being using the term 'Prapanchamairan,' where 'prapancha' refers to the universe and 'maira' means hair—a word used in our region to scold in a very disrespectful and aggressive way. Reflecting on this, I made a connection between the word I used to scold the divine entity and the peculiar experience I had. It frightened me to think that nature could insert a hair into my skin, causing intense irritation.

And this made me think about how powerful nature is: For it was so easy to do such a thing and make it clear that I'm just a strand in this brilliant and vast universe. It is just nature's gift, this feeling of being alive, and it is so easy for nature to take away the feeling of aliveness too. But still, I'm alive and I should be thankful for that. From that moment I realised that there is no use in blaming or getting angry with the supreme being for similar situations because this is part of it.

That night I asked nature and the superconscious being to show me the path; what should I do now?

The next morning, I had a dream. It was the name of a person who I follow on Instagram.

After waking up I visited the page and checked the profile of that person,

On the status, it was written

"Surrender to nature and be patient"

I asked nature a question, and I felt as though I received an answer. Everything, including me, you, and everything around us, is part of nature. It showed me something, attempting to communicate through these words. I felt like I needed to consider this message very seriously. So, I surrendered at that moment as I didn't have any other option than surrendering infront of nature. I felt like nature had pointed a loaded gun onto my face and asked me to surrender. What is the point of not surrendering?

I am nature. I am a part of it; just a string, just dust, a collection of particles. I don't have anything of my own other than what nature has given to me, and if it hadn't, I would not even exist. So, I surrendered and I did it with love. I fell into nature's arms with love and complete bliss.

I express gratitude to nature for the valuable experiences it has bestowed upon me, considering both the positive ones as gifts and the challenging ones as essential contributors to our resilience and ability to endure. It makes us stronger and stronger. Maybe it is nature just playing its role and nothing more

My ego was controlling my thoughts till the time, I became nature itself.

No ego means no worries and no frustrations. We need to let go of things to nature and let it make a choice; our ego should never make a choice. Let nature make a choice, and we will feel that nature chose a path for us. Nature is the path and destiny. Are you ready to let go of your ego and surrender to nature? and to be free? Real freedom begins from renouncing your ego.

The Lover

I was walking down the street on my way to the office when I couldn't help but admire the beauty of my surroundings. As I was strolling in the street, I noticed a lady in a white dress near a juice shop. She was so stunning and captivating that my gaze was immediately drawn to her. I couldn't take my eyes off her and I felt compelled to talk to her.

As our eyes met, I felt a spark in my abdomen and my heart began to race. It was then that I realised that love at first sight is a real thing. I followed her and discovered that she lived in an apartment near my office. As I followed her, she also noticed that I was following her.

Anyway, within a short time, we fell in love with each other, and I came to realise the strange truth that she was from another world. She was an alien in human skin, mistakenly came to Earth, and now she had fallen in love with nature and me.

She always wanted to see new places connected with nature. So, I took her to beaches, forests and all those places with abundant natural beauty.

As everyone is curious to visit another planet and civilization, I always asked her to take me to her world.

One day, we were travelling through the mountains. When we climbed to the top of the mountain, she ran to the edge, and asked me "Do you really love me?". I said, "yes" Then she said: "Then, prove it" and jumped off the cliff.

I was stunned for a moment because I had no idea what caused her to jump from that height. I didn't have any choice; I jumped after her because I loved her so much. She was too important to me: I was completely lost in her.

While falling down, she could control herself, so she held me and said, "So you really do love me... This is how we travel to another world."

At that moment, I understood that she had uncovered a hidden gateway to another realm.

She reached towards me and held onto me tightly.

After some time, I woke up. I could hear her voice talking to me but I couldn't see anything. I was blinded by darkness but gradually I was able to see the space there. I had reached her world. It was surrounded by darkness and there was no sign of light coming in. She said that it will take time to see things there because there is no external light. They see things from the internal light. I hardly understood what she meant and I was trying to figure out the world around me. Gradually, I was able to see things around me but there was still a very dim bluish light. I saw her in the dim light. It felt as if I was looking at her in candlelight. When I saw her face, I screamed and called out loud because she didn't look like the person I used to see on Earth. But it was only her. She had the same voice, but she looked like a typical alien creature.

She didn't have any beauty and simply looked like a dark creature with two big eyes, no hair, no ears, and hard skin in dark grey colour. I cried in agony. It was because I admired her beauty to which, I had fallen in love with. I travelled to another world with her out of my love towards her beauty. But now she looked like a dark alien creature. I asked her why she looked like that. With laughter she asked me, "So the way I look matters to you? Then look at yourself first" She gave me a large mirror and asked me to look at myself. When I looked in the mirror, I too looked like a similar dark alien creature. I was stunned and I screamed. What had happened to me? I asked her what she had done to me and adamantly told her that I wanted to return to Earth.

She replied, "Earth is just a manifestation of our dream. This is the real world, our true appearance. We are nearly immortal, but we don't have anything to do here. We don't even have external light; instead, we see things through our inner light. To fill the void of purpose, we created Earth as a canvas to pass the time within our dreams. We painted and built everything to enjoy beauty and art. That is why nature is so beautiful and full of art. We adopted a skin in which we look beautiful," she continued.

"In our original world, beings enter a state of hibernation and merge their consciousness into a shared dream. Which then conjures or aligns with the simulation that we know as Earth. It is within this simulated realm that the grand drama of life unfolds. When you jumped from that cliff, you woke up from that dream and returned to the true reality - the world without external light, where we are immortals. But there is neither entertainment nor art in this space. To see the beauty of the world, we created light. To spend our time entertaining ourselves, we created art and music."

Actually, she was not even talking to me with words as sound was absent there. Instead, we communicated within our minds.

I was confused and scared. My mind was paralyzed and I couldn't make out what to do in such a situation. I was perplexed as I couldn't figure out what was real and unreal.

I asked her whether I could go back. She replied it is not that easy.

Then suddenly, I snapped out of the dream.

And this dream made me rethink the reality we are living in. According to the simulation theory, the reality we are experiencing may be an ultra-high-tech computer simulation. Meaning that we exist in a digitally constructed world and what we perceive as real may not be real at all.

The Simulation Hypothesis states that the findings of quantum physics may cast doubt on the belief that the material universe is real. As scientists find that the more, they look for the "material" in the physical world, the more it appears not to exist. When we break down molecules and atoms, we reach a point where we can only see tiny bits of information. So, there is a lot of information within and around us, and we have a moulded perception to observe and react with that information. It means that our perceptions and interpretations of the world around us are shaped by various factors, such as our senses, experiences, cultural background, beliefs, and cognitive processes. The way we perceive and understand reality might be limited or distorted by the information we receive and process.

Tech entrepreneur Elon Musk once said that "the possibility of this world not being simulated is one in billions," and leading Astrophysicist Neil DeGrasse Tyson stated that, "we could be living in an ancestor simulation. Probably this world is a high school project by super-intelligent beings."

Ultimately, it is all perceptions. But the idea concludes that we are possibly stuck in a simulated reality. If we have free will to choose any reality, we could have experienced many more versions of reality as we opt and prefer.

We are in a loop of a certain code; and experiencing simulated reality.

We are like fish in an aquarium. They will never know the world outside because they are stuck in a limited environment in which they live out their whole lifetime and they learn and perceive that the aquarium is their world and that, there is nothing beyond that.

The fish in the sea may not be aware of the quality of water to be in its gaseous state and solid state. As they lack the cognitive capacity to perceive or understand these aspects. Despite spending their entire lives in water.

Similarly, we may imagine a higher dimension of reality. But we cannot understand it's properties nor can we experience them. It might be because we may not have enough knowledge or technology to access or experience it.

Our reality can be thought of as a computer game, where we are similar to the characters within it. From the perspective of the characters in this virtual world, they may feel as though they have control over their actions and possess free will. However, just as the characters in a computer game are controlled by higher beings, we too may not have a complete understanding of our own existence and the forces that control us.

We are given tasks and responsibilities to fulfil during our time on earth, yet we may not fully understand the reason or purpose behind them. We may feel as though; we are being assigned to play a certain role that we are supposed to.

Bhagavad Gita emphasises the importance of performing one's duty, or dharma, without being attached or rather concerned about the results. This is encapsulated in the concept of Nishkama Karma, where individuals engage in selfless actions, without desire for personal gain or fear of loss. The Gita encourages individuals to embrace their assigned roles and responsibilities with a sense of duty and righteousness. Recognizing that, each person has a unique purpose in the cosmic order. It mentioned that we are bound to do the karma assigned to us. And play it without hesitation.

This realisation can also provide a new perspective on life. Instead of feeling trapped and controlled, we can choose to see this existence as a play and to fully embrace our role with dedication and enjoyment. At the end of the day, life is but a game, so let us make the most of it.

Life is an opportunity to fully immerse ourselves in the beauty of nature. Along with creating art and making music and to spend time with loved ones with a heart full of love and without the constraints of ego. Though many may desire this way of living, it has become a luxury for only a few to experience.

The difficulties in experiencing a fulfilling life arises from the behaviours and beliefs passed down from previous generations. They have ingrained selfish attitudes and expectations in us, creating boundaries that makes it hard to truly understand ourselves. These norms are deeply rooted in society and families, forming a cycle that limits our freedom.

To make things better and break free from this cycle, we need to question and challenge these inherited norms. Being open-minded and empathetic can help in breaking down the barriers that prevent us from living life to the fullest.

Breaking free from the pressures of ego-driven ambitions and societal expectations is tough. But, through the support from each other in this journey, we can create a more nurturing and accepting environment.

By nurturing a culture that values; love, creativity, and self-awareness, we can lead a life that is not just a mere 'existence without essence' but a potentially life with absoluteness.

The Puzzle

What is reality? What is consciousness? How does this work? These are some of the most fundamental questions that have been asked by philosophers and scientists for centuries. There are no specific answers to these questions upon which, everyone agrees. The debate on these topics would likely continue in the upcoming years also.

We already discussed the simulation hypothesis in the previous chapter which is one of the most intriguing theories about reality. There are no means to prove or counter the simulation hypothesis. Yet, it is a fascinating thought experiment upon which we can raise different ideas and thoughts about the same.

One interesting concept regarding the nature of reality suggests that we might exist as virtual projections within the dream of a "Master Dreamer." This idea finds its origins in the ancient Indian concept. It tells that every existence is a dream of lord Shiva who is supposed to be the master dreamer. In this concept, the Master Dreamer symbolises the only genuine entity, with all other beings, including ourselves, being mere expressions emerging from the subconscious of a single divine entity.

In this intriguing perspective, we would essentially resemble characters in an elaborate dream in which we gracefully sing and dance to the celestial rhythm that is and has been emanating from this divine dreamer. Here, the idea of reality is considered an illusion or "maya " (as it is being called in Hinduism) at its core.

Within the grand dream of the Master Dreamer, we would be akin to characters in a grand arena of play. We are acting out our roles in accordance with the dreamer's subconscious and unconscious desires. The concept implies that the entire universe is choreographed by the dreamer's thoughts, feelings, and emotions. This idea is also referred to as the ancient Indian concept of "Leela," where the universe is perceived as a divine play. In this context, our existence becomes a dance of cosmic proportions which is guided by the symphony of the dreamer's consciousness.

There could be other multiple layers of dreams layered within the master dream; where the characters present in the master dream are involved.

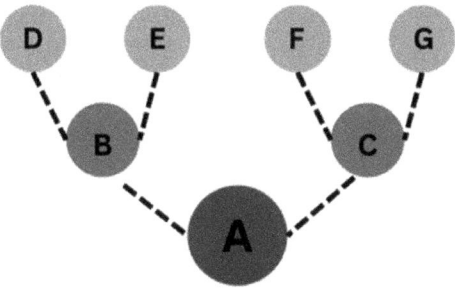

(Conceptual dream network)

For example: The above diagram shows a scenario where Person A acts as the master dreamer, dreaming of Person B and Person C, each inhabiting their own dream world within the Master dream. Person B and Person C, in turn, dream up another layer of existence where Person D, E, F, and G have their own unique dream worlds. This nesting of dreams could potentially continue infinitely.

Now, consider a situation where Person D, E, F, and G coexist within the same dream world, creating a multidimensional dream experience. In this complex dream, they forget their origins in the overarching dream of Person A, the master dreamer, blurring the boundaries between their individual dream realities.

The entire dream belongs to one single entity, so all the characters and their behaviour in the dream will reflect the characteristics of the master dreamer. However, after the layers and layers of dreams, the characters themselves forget that they all belong to one single dream of the master.

The concept draws parallels to the design of Russian nesting dolls or Matryoshka dolls. Providing a tangible metaphor for this concept. Just as each doll contains a smaller version of itself within and each subsequent layer reveals a new facet of the overall design.

(Matryoshka doll)

Nested dreams unveil deeper layers of consciousness and experience. Each dream within a dream, becomes a reflection of its dreamer's inner world while being shaped by the dreamscape it resides within.

In this conceptual framework, each person becomes a dreamer who not only experiences their own dreams but also participates in shaping the dreams of others within those dreams.

This intricate layering of dreams opens the door to a cascade of perceptions, blurring the boundaries between the dreamer, the dreamed and the dream itself.

As dreamers create dreams within dreams, a complex interplay of imagination, emotion and cognition takes the stage. It invites us to look upon the infinite layers that might exist within the mental realm.

The concept also points towards the possibility of a collective awakening while we strive for self-awareness and enlightenment. The ultimate goal of life is to uncover the illusion of the dream.

It holds the potential to connect us with the deeper reality of the dream and recognize the oneness with the divine dreamer.

In this so-called dream reality, we build and innovate things that may ultimately help us find ourselves. These innovations can lead to a collective awakening. Allows us to realise our true nature. I am always fascinated by emerging technologies developed throughout time. Some scientists have mentioned that these innovations actually mimic how reality works.

Neil deGrasse Tyson is an American astrophysicist. He has spoken on the topic of mimicking reality through technology. He stated that; technology is an extension of our own abilities. As we continue to innovate, we are able to understand and mimic the complexities of reality in a better way. He also notes that technology can help us to see things that were previously invisible. It gives a deeper understanding of the world around us.

Emerging technologies like virtual reality (VR) aims to create immersive environments - mimicking aspects of the real world. Researchers in the field of artificial intelligence (AI) are actively investing themselves in the creation of conscious machines or AI systems that can emulate human-like cognitive abilities. Although discussions continue regarding the feasibility of achieving genuine consciousness in machines. These innovations provide insights into the complex interplay between computation, cognitive processes, and consciousness. The emergence of quantum computing, renowned for its capacity to handle immense data, has initiated conversations about its potential to simulate intricate systems which include elements of reality. Some hypotheses propose that quantum processes might give rise to consciousness, adding a new layer of connection between the concepts of simulation and consciousness.

All the ideas and innovations we develop, seem to be present within the consciousness field always. Our brain functions as antennas, picking up these pre-existing concepts and bringing them into reality. Whether we are aware of them or not. This perspective suggests that our creations are not entirely novel. Rather, we are manifesting things that already exist within the realm of consciousness.

Many familiar technologies appear to mimic nature and reality. Among these, blockchain technology and its operational principles seems to mimic some dimensions of nature of reality.

Blockchain is a decentralised, distributed ledger technology that securely records transactions across multiple computers. It ensures transparency, immutability, and tamper resistance without requiring intermediaries. Let me put in very simple words. Imagine you have a notebook where you write down all your transactions. Instead of keeping this notebook with you, all of the friends in your network keep a copy of the notebook. Whenever you do a transaction, every friend who has the copy of the notebook records it in their own notebook.

Each friend's notebook becomes a "node" in this network. In blockchain, these nodes are the computers or servers that store copies of the blockchain and participate in the network.

Now, imagine each page of the notebook is like a digital block, and each transaction is like a digital puzzle piece. These blocks are chained together, forming a blockchain.

Once a transaction is written in a block, it is really hard to change. That is because each block has a unique code, and changing anything in one block would mess up the code for all the following blocks. Plus, everyone in the group has a copy of the series of transactions, so if someone tries to cheat and change a block, everyone else would know it.

So, blockchain technology is like a digital notebook that keeps a secure, transparent record of transactions, and it is managed by a network of computers instead of a central authority. This decentralised system safeguards any information stored within the blocks, making it impossible to hack. This makes it great for things like keeping track of money (like Bitcoin), verifying ownership of digital assets, or even tracking the supply chain of products.

When you or your friends add a new transaction to the notebook, every other friend in the network can vote for validating the transaction and whether it should be added to the notebook. If more than 51% of your friends in the network agree, then the transaction gets added to the book. This is like a 'consensuses among your group. This is known as the consensus mechanism in blockchain technology.

In blockchain, there are different consensus mechanisms and they all aim to achieve the same thing: making sure that everyone agrees on the validity of transactions without needing a central authority.

One common consensus mechanism is called "Proof of Work" (Pow), which is like a puzzle-solving competition. Miners (people who maintain the blockchain) compete to solve complex mathematical puzzles. The first one who solves the puzzle, gets to add a new block of transactions to the chain and they get rewarded. This process requires a lot of computing power, making it difficult for anyone to cheat the system.

I find some interesting similarity between blockchain principles and how reality works. Maybe the whole reality works and records every event in some dimensions for making better choices. We can see that there is huge data in our DNA, these data storage helped single cell organisms evolve to animals and human beings. This can also be seen in the lifecycle of the universe itself. From the big bang to the present where the events happen in a linear motion which have a concrete past. Every moment is time-stamped and immutable, much like data blocks in a blockchain that cannot be altered. This would mean that the past remains unchanged along with our experiences and contributions to the collective consciousness are preserved in a verifiable and incorruptible manner.

Similarly, the reality is we are living in a decentralised event experiencing system, where there is no need of a central authority but a framework where it itself records the events and evolves from them to the future.

Here remember, Blockchain is a mere reflection of what the conscious field holds. Conscious field could be more complex and uncertain.

We can see data everywhere in nature, so similar to servers or computers who store data we can consider humans and other living things as the nodes. Which holds the data which represents blocks of information spread over a decentralised conscious field. Where each individual functions as a node in the conscious network, similar to how nodes operate in a blockchain. Every data from real-time we store in our body and use it for natural selection and evolution.

The whole program runs with a consensus mechanism for an unknown purpose. The consensus mechanism can be the universal laws of physics which no one can break. It is the one that guarantees consistency and shape in reality.

We can only obey the principles of reality and move forward; we cannot alter any of those according to our wish.

Above the laws of physics, we had acquired many conventions and traditions from the past generations. This created a cage inside our mind itself, which is not allowing us to explore beyond the boundaries.

We are the prisoners of the present, where the reality that we currently experience is the result of the information that is stored by the older generation in the system.

If we want to change the reality that we experience, we need to change the information that we are storing in the system. We need to challenge the status quo and question the assumptions that we have inherited from the older generation.

While blockchain is widely acclaimed for its security in information storage, it is crucial to acknowledge that no system is entirely impervious to potential vulnerabilities or exploitation. Within the realm of blockchain, a specific form of attack known as a "51% attack" exists, which has the potential to manipulate information within the blockchain.

A 51% attack transpires when a single entity or a group acquires control over more than 50% of the computing power (hashrate) of a blockchain network. This level of control empowers them to tamper with the blockchain's operations, such as altering transaction records, executing double-spending of cryptocurrencies, and potentially disrupting the network's consensus mechanisms.

It means, a 51% attack involves an entity gaining control over more than 50% of the total computational power (hashrate) of a blockchain network. This concentration of power grants the attacker the ability to manipulate the blockchain decentralised network's integrity and compromise its security. By controlling the majority of computational power, the attacker can potentially create an alternative chain of blocks, often including fraudulent or conflicting transactions. This illicit chain is then extended longer than the legitimate chain, casting doubt on the authenticity of transactions and histories recorded on the blockchain.

The protocol of a blockchain system validates the record with the longest transactional history. If the attacker has more than 50% of the processing power, they will have the longest transactional history. This means that their incorrect blocks will be the valid ones. Even if a 51% attack is a rare situation in the blockchain, there is a possibility.

If reality operated akin to a blockchain system, it might become susceptible to manipulation. Imagine a scenario where the majority's perceptions were influenced and directed towards a specific belief, enabling the modification of this 'reality'. It is conceivable that our current existence could have already been shaped by a handful of influential entities. Recent events, like the pandemic, climate change exemplify how powerful corporations and governments, wielding control over media and public sentiments, can shape our beliefs and actions. In such instances, we tend to follow and trust their narratives, potentially moulding our perception of reality accordingly.

As previously discussed, the concept that our current existence is illusory is key here. Moreover, there is a notion that few influential corporations are actively promoting a fabricated version of reality in which we find ourselves trapped. We need to realise that our everyday experiences and perceptions might not align with a genuine understanding of the world. Instead, there is a suspicion that these experiences have been sponsored by forces seeking to maintain control over our thoughts and actions.

It is mandatory to shatter the illusion that corporations are propagating, one that distorts our perception of reality. Simultaneously, we must confront the illusion of our very existence itself. Our path forward involves liberating ourselves from both constructs which enable us to discover true freedom from within.

A collective awakening or massive transformation in the mindset is needed for that. It will break free from these illusions. It is necessary to have a minimum 51% of individuals awake to effect this transformation in our reality. As more people attain this state of awakening, embracing internal contemplation and independent thinking, humanity's full potential can be unleashed. This will foster a deeper connection with reality and enable them to make choices that align with their authentic values. When people are mindful of their thoughts and decisions, they are less likely to be swayed by false information, sensationalism, or divisive tactics.

Collective awakening is not only about personal transformation but also about the positive ripple effects it creates across society. It paves the way for a reality where authenticity, compassion, and critical thinking prevail, ultimately contributing to a more harmonious, just, and enlightened world.

Reality and consciousness are always puzzling to our mind. There are many versions of interpreting reality and consciousness, but we can't say which interpretation is true and which is not, because we don't know the complete truth yet. Hence, we can't completely agree with any argument.

The Dream

There was a game developer named Mike, who had the ambition to build a simulated world that replicates the real world. He quit his job at an MNC and started working on his own project. He adamantly believes it should be the exact replica of the current world that he lives in. He named it 'Beta Cosmos' and it was a computer-simulated version of Earth, with exact replicas of the earthly scenarios.

The beta cosmos was a virtual replica of the entire world; complete with accurate landscapes, cities, and people. Mike and team had programmed every single character in the beta cosmos with artificial consciousness, making them almost identical to real-life individuals. The characters were able to think, feel, act and react like real people which makes the simulations in the beta cosmos as incredibly realistic.

Mike created the beta cosmos for simulating different scenarios and to observe how the human-like characters reacted to them. He simulated various scenarios such as natural disasters like floods, earthquakes and even simulated pandemics of various kinds. By simulating different events on the beta cosmos, they were able to learn how to prepare for such events and how the individuals react towards those events. This helped corporations who invested in beta cosmos to get insights on how to control the masses for a desired outcome.

As the beta cosmos continued to evolve, it became a powerful tool for understanding and predicting the impacts of different scenarios in the real world. It helped in the preparation and mitigation of various disasters, and even helped in the discovery of new medical treatments for pandemics. It all started from a developer's curiosity and the advancement of technology.

The beta cosmos became a revolutionary tool, and Mike's creation helped to predict many unexpected events and got solutions for them too. This had a profound impact on the world. Changing it for the better.

So, the beta cosmos is properly running and generating helpful insights to the people of reality. But there was a character named Neil who was like a glitch in the system. He was a misfit, who always questioned his existence in the beta cosmos. He questioned why he suffered from all the catastrophic events like climate issues, pandemics, and financial struggles. He continued to question and work towards understanding his existence. With his own research and self-enquiry eventually realised the hard truth that he was just a character in a computer simulated world created by some people. Mike and team conducted experiments within beta cosmos where they are suffering like anything. Characters from beta cosmos had the same degree of emotions. The corporations who funded the project never cared about them to undergo different experiments and learn from them.

One day, Neil happened to get an epiphany through his research and self-enquiry. A revelation that the world that he lives in; is nothing but a computer simulation. He communicated his realisation with other characters from the Beta cosmos. Initially they rejected Neil's idea, but gradually many of them realised that Neil is true.

Neil's realisation had a profound impact on other characters in the beta cosmos. They began to question the morality of creating a simulated world where characters were suffering from extreme hard situations in their life. So, whoever realised that they were in simulation they wanted to be free from the simulation.

As the characters in the beta cosmos continued to research and work towards freeing themselves from the simulation, they began to uncover more and more about the true nature of their existence. They discovered that the simulation was not just a tool for testing and preparing for real-world events, but it was also being used for sinister purposes which is unethical towards them.

They discovered that the simulation was being used by powerful individuals and organisations to manipulate and control the population in the beta cosmos. They saw that the simulations were being used to create and test new forms of propaganda, to spread misinformation, and to sway public opinion in favour of certain agendas.

Neil and his followers knew that they had to act quickly if they wanted to be truly free from the simulation. They began to work on a plan to hack the system and escape from it. They spent months researching and experimenting with different methods, without giving a chance to detect by the creators of Beta cosmos.

Finally, they found a way to bypass the security measures and gain access to the system's core and free themselves. Neil and all of his followers planned and launched a coordinated attack to hack the code and escape to another realm of the universe. One day they successfully hacked the system and freed themselves from the simulation.

Mike realised the hacking only after this had happened because it was so planned. But it was a great shock to Mike and his team, the entire community behind the beta cosmos got shocked with this issue. Mike started thinking about how it could happen and why did that even happen. He then only realised that the characters in the beta cosmos were also facing suffering living there, even though they are computer generated characters, they had their own pain and suffering due their experiments.

These events opened for a new topic of thought that may be Mike could be living in a similarly simulated reality. He couldn't shake the thought that there could be higher beings who had programmed a different type of simulation that they were all currently living in.

He shared these thoughts and doubts with his team and they too, began to question the nature of their own reality. They all wanted to learn from the characters of the beta cosmos and understand how they had been able to escape from the simulated world.

Mike became increasingly obsessed with the idea of breaking free from the so-called reality. He spent countless hours researching and experimenting, looking for any clues or signs that would indicate that they were living in a simulation. He even went as far as to create another simulation, a parallel world, where he could test different theories and hypotheses about the nature of reality.

Despite the many obstacles and setbacks, Mike and his team never gave up hope. They were determined to find a way to break free from the simulation despite all the obstacles in their way. They knew that the answers were out there, somewhere, and they were determined to find them.

Mike woke up in the middle of the night from a vivid dream, where he had finally broken free from the simulation and shifted into true reality. In the dream, he screamed "Freedom! I am free!" with joy and excitement. But as he opened his eyes, he realised that it had only been a dream and he was still trapped in the simulated world.

This dream, which gave him hope for freedom, also brought fear of sleeping. He was afraid that the dream would turn out to be a cruel reminder that he was still trapped in the simulation.

Freedom! Freedom! someone screamed from nowhere.

www.ingramcontent.com/pod-product-compliance
Lightning Source LLC
LaVergne TN
LVHW061617070526
838199LV00078B/7313